# FOREIGN MARRIAGE

*A Modern Day Saga of the Woman at the Well*

Alotha Jené Mayes

www.TrueVinePublishing.org

Foreign Marriage
Alotha Jené Mayes

Published by
True Vine Publishing Co.
810 Dominican Dr.
Nashville, TN 37228
www.TrueVinePublishing.org

Copyright © 2025 by Alotha Jené Mayes
All rights reserved. No part of this book may be reproduced in any form or by any electronic or mechanical means, including information storage and retrieval or mechanical means without permission in writing from the publisher, except by a reviewer who may quote brief passages in a review.

*Scripture quotations taken from the King James Version. Public domain.*

*Scripture quotations taken from the Holy Bible, New International Version®, NIV®. Copyright © 1973, 1978, 1984, 2011 by Biblica, Inc.™ Used by permission. All rights reserved worldwide.*

ISBN: 978-1-968092-39-9 Paperback
ISBN: 978-1-968092-40-5 eBook

Printed in the United States—First printing

For more information about the author, go to www.alothajmayes.com

# DEDICATION

To AlothaBread

You were not wrong to believe that love begets love. You only needed to know that loving yourself first and knowing how to do so was the key.

"I was one way…and now I am completely different. And the thing that happened in between… was Him."

~Mary Magdalene The Chosen (S1:E2)

Thank you, Lord, for being there for me.

**~Psalm 139:8**

# ACKNOWLEDGEMENTS

To my sister, the **Alsum, Whitney Brooke Snell,** thank you for being my why. From the moment you were born, when I was just nine years old, you became my reason to keep going, to keep striving, and to keep searching for what was right and good.

Thank you for always following me, even when I was headed in the wrong direction. Thank you for believing in me and doing your best to keep us together as a family.

I love you forever. You will always be my number one.

To my friends, **Denita Milliner, Kathy Stripling-Terrell,** and every other person who has ever uttered the words, *"Girl, you should write a book,"* thank you.

Denita, you believed I could do it even when you didn't really know me, and that belief touched me more deeply than you could have imagined. Your words, and the faith behind them, planted a seed of courage that helped bring this book to life.

I am forever grateful to each of you who saw something in me before I saw it in myself.

To my beautiful sisters in Christ, **Lorria Anderson, Jamese Cherry, Nina Davis-Harmon, Karyl Kirkland, Felicia Piper, and Schuronda Scott**, thank you for being my prayer warriors, encouragers, and truth-tellers throughout this publishing journey. When I was nervous, second-guessing myself, and afraid of being judged, you reminded me that this book wasn't about perfection, it was about purpose.

You prayed over me, spoke life into my spirit, and reminded me that what God starts, He always finishes. Your faith in me helped me stand when I felt like shrinking back, and your love reminded me that I was never walking this road alone.

This book carries pieces of each of you, your strength, your prayers, your laughter, and your unwavering belief in what God was doing through me. I thank God for you, and I love you beyond words.

To **Timothy Bond** of **True Vine Publishing**, from the very beginning of our contract, our connection has felt more like a friendship than a business relationship. From our first conversation, it was as if I'd known you since elementary school. I truly believe God handpicked you to bring this book to life.

Your obedience to His voice is what sets you apart. Whatever God tells you to say, whether it's a word of encouragement, correction, or direction, you say it with love and conviction. There were moments in this process when I felt like I was talking directly to God Himself, hearing His reminders through you: that this is not *my* project, not simply the telling of *my* story, but *His*.

Through your guidance, I've come to see this book as a testimony of God's grace and mercy, proof that He can bring beauty out of any situation, no matter how hopeless it may seem. Just as Jesus said of Lazarus, "This happened so that the glory of God might be revealed." That is what this project has become: a reflection of His glory, told through His vessel and brought to life through your obedience.

Thank you, Timothy, for walking in your calling and allowing God to use you to help me walk in mine.

To the men I've hurt, the wives whose marriages I disrupted, and most of all, my children, I offer my deepest and sincerest apologies for the pain I caused and the harmful example I set. I carry that awareness with humility and deep regret, fully owning the choices that caused so much hurt.

Yet by God's grace and mercy, I have been forgiven and transformed. I have learned, I have healed, and I have forgiven myself. My prayer is that, in time, you can find it in your hearts to forgive me, too.

*"If we confess our sins, he is faithful and just and will forgive us our sins and purify us from all unrighteousness."*
*~1 John 1:9*

These are my confessions.

# PROLOGUE

This is chaos! I feel like I'm caught in the middle of a tornado, clinging to a thin pole, or maybe I'm sliding into a pit, desperately digging in my fingernails to keep from being pulled under. I know You are with me, God. *"Your rod and Your staff, they comfort me."* But I still feel so alone. So lost.

I know You want me to truly cast my cares on You, to surrender, but I have spent my entire life clinging to the illusion of control. It's funny, really, none of us is truly in control of anything, yet we fight so hard to hold on. To what? What exactly am I trying to grasp so desperately?

If I'm honest, I think I'm just trying to keep bad things from happening. *"All my life, I had to fight!"* Long before Oprah Winfrey made those words famous, I was already fighting to live, to survive an existence my parents never wanted for me.

I am here on a dare.

In the Mid-1960s, the United States was at the pinnacle of the Civil Rights Movement. Names like Dr. Martin Luther King, Jr, Angela Davis, Malcolm X, and Rosa Parks graced the headlines as they battled for the fundamental human (civil) rights of people of color. Segregation and integration were the topics of many hot-seated debates.

Activists marched, preached, and protested. Some musicians used their platforms to create music to support these protests. Like the 1968 James Brown hit, *Say It Loud, I'm Black, and I'm Proud*. And while most minorities fought with the civil rights leaders, some of a lighter complexion chose to "pass."

"Racial passing occurs when a person classified as a member of a racial group is accepted or perceived ("passes") as a member of another." In short, not many African Americans were proud to be black, especially those of a darker complexion, like my mother. Even within the black community, the darker your complexion, the more scrutiny you fell under. Only those of a lighter complexion were considered attractive (fine). My mother so desired to be with my father because, according to these standards, he was fine simply because he was light-skinned.

My father told my mother he would only be her boyfriend if she had sex with him. So, on a cold January day in 1966, she skipped school and gave him her virginity in one of the very houses I would later grow up in. When she discovered she was pregnant, she was terrified and devastated. Like any scared young girl, she made several desperate attempts to end the pregnancy, drinking an entire bottle of liquor, throwing herself down the stairs, anything to make it all go away. But nothing worked. Much to her dismay, early one Sunday morning in September of that same year, I was born. My mother and father were only sixteen years old.

My grandmother named me after her younger sister, a woman she deeply admired. She was proud of all her ten siblings, but there was something special about Alotha Colleen. Beautiful, intelligent, strong, and determined, she carried herself with grace and purpose. She was organized, she could cook, and her fair skin seemed to glow against the soft light of her presence. To me, she was the most beautiful of them all.

As I grew older, I began to understand what an honor it was to bear her name. But as a child, I hated it. *Alotha* was different, uncommon, and being different made me stand out.

My nickname came about shortly after I was born. Some of my mother's high school friends came by to see the new baby, and when they heard my name, one of them laughed and said, *"Alotha? That sounds like a loaf of bread."* For some reason, my grandmother thought that was cute, and just like that, I became *"AlothaBread."*

My mother was an only child. Her parents tried many times, but she was the only one to survive. There was at least one miscarriage before and after her birth. My grandmother was heartbroken. Combined with the fact that she always wanted a boy child, my mother was the spitting image of my grandfather. She was a "Daddy's Girl," and my grandmother hated it. She often referred to her as "Mama's Little Black Baby," including introductions.

*"Hello, I'm Willa, and this is Andii, my little black baby,"* she would say. As a result, my mother developed a negative self-image that she would carry until the day she

died. But not before ensuring that her two daughters saw themselves through those exact same lenses.

Due to my father's light skin, I inherited the same complexion as my grandmother. This brought her much joy, and she was extremely vocal in her delight. Now, I don't ever remember her complimenting my appearance or anything else, for that matter. But my mother often lamented about how "color struck' my grandmother was and reflected on the comments she would make that confirmed the idea.

"Color Struck is an old saying among African-Americans that refers to individuals who believe that a lighter complexion and European features represent the epitome of beauty and desirability." My grandmother reinforced to my mother that because of her complexion, she would never consider her attractive in any way, and because of that, she was not deserving of the unconditional love that should flow from a mother to her child, particularly a child that she struggled to bring into the world.

Imagine the bitterness that must have burned within my mother when the child that she didn't want (me) showed up looking just like the mother who didn't want her. I am convinced that my mother has resented me, and I will go as far as to say, hated me from the very first day.

I was in her way. I was a hindrance to her high school teenager/young adult lifestyle. As the unwanted child of teenage parents, and for almost ten years, the only child, no one, except maybe my father's sister, wanted to be bothered with me, and they made sure that I knew it.

*"You get on my damn nerves!"* or *"Get yo' dumb ass somewhere and sit down!"* are a few phrases I would often hear. *"Why you ask so many damn questions?"*

Then, there was my all-time favorite, *"What do you think I had you for?"* This one was used in response to any opposition to a personal service request from my mother. I was well into adulthood before I realized that God had placed me here for reasons that had nothing to do with bidding my mother's every request.

When I wasn't being yelled at for possessing childlike behaviors as a child, it was being reinforced that not only was I unwanted, but that I wasn't very attractive or intelligent. Nappy-headed, skinny, foolish, lazy, all terms that were frequently used. My mother often celebrated that I was taking inanity to an all-time high with the phrase, *"You practice being stupid!"*

Those words still ring in my head. Even though she has been dead for over 17 years, occasionally, I can still hear many of her words. *"You just like yo' daddy! You ain't never gon' be nothing!"*

But I didn't have my "daddy." Instead, I had Skeet. Skeet was my stepfather, an abusive, mean-spirited alcoholic whose presence filled the house with unease.

I think I hated Skeet from the very beginning, though I wouldn't have admitted it at the time. Back then, I was just a little girl desperate for a father. For as long as I can remember, mine was off somewhere, living his best life, or so I thought. Although they were married when I was a toddler, I don't ever remember my parents living together.

I wanted–no, I needed–someone to bring balance to our chaotic household, someone to offer love and gentleness in a life that had very little of either. It was just Mama and me, and though she tolerated me, she did it out of obligation, not affection.

There were fleeting moments of care, but they were rare enough that I clung to them like sparks in the dark. Mostly, I learned early that I was an inconvenience, a presence to be managed rather than cherished.

When Skeet came into our lives, I allowed myself a flicker of hope. I was sitting on the front porch in one of my summer outfits, school just let out, the air thick with the promise of long, free days. I noticed a man coming out of the house next door. For a moment, I thought, "That's my daddy!" My heart leapt.

He wasn't my father, though at first glance, he bore just enough resemblance to him that my heart leapt with hope. Skeet looked so much like my father that people often mistake my sister– Skeet's daughter with my mother– for my twin. The sting of disappointment washed over me, but that fleeting spark of hope, that moment when I thought I might finally see him, marked the beginning of everything that would follow.

In the weeks after that, Skeet lingered. Conversations with my mother grew longer. Before long, he was living with us. Soon after, my mother became pregnant, and they married. That's when everything changed for the worse.

At first, I clung to the hope that Skeet might become the father I had longed for. I even asked him if I could call him "Daddy." His answer was flat, dismissive: *"No. I've already got too many kids."*

I didn't understand then, but I learned quickly. Four younger children from his previous relationships began visiting, and the household suddenly became crowded and chaotic.

I was no longer a child in a home; I was the oldest, the caretaker, the scapegoat. Broken plates, spilled drinks, or misplaced toys became my responsibility. If something went wrong, I was punished. If one of the younger children cried, I was blamed.

The punishments weren't always subtle. I remember a Saturday afternoon, sitting on the couch, watching television, trying to disappear. Skeet and my mother were arguing in the bedroom. Their voices rose, the words sharp, slicing through the calm of the living room. The door burst open.

*"LoafaBread! Bring me a belt!"*

I froze. I knew that tone; it meant trouble. My hands shook as I obeyed, fetching the belt. I had thought I would be the one to receive it, but instead, he took it into the bedroom. The door slammed. Moments later came the sounds that would imprint on me forever: the crack of leather against skin, my mother's desperate screams, and a terrified plea. *"Stop, Skeet! Please stop!"*

I ran to my room, closed the door, sat on the bed, knees tucked to my chest, and prayed for it to end. When it did, the silence was heavier than the violence that caused it.

That day, I realized the father I had dreamed of, the safe, loving presence I had hoped for, would never exist in the form I had imagined. Skeet wasn't the protector I craved. He was a predator in my home, and the cycle of abuse began in earnest: if he wasn't hitting my mother, he was hitting me, and if he wasn't hitting me, she was. If a child cried, a toy broke, or a chore went undone, I bore the weight of it all.

Looking back now, I understand that my hatred for Skeet wasn't personal in the way I thought it was as a child. It was a response to the broken promise he represented: the father I never had, the safety that never came, the love that was conditional at best. My mother's resentment and reluctant tolerance would at times flicker into moments of care, but beneath it all lay a quiet, simmering disdain that deepened the pain. It shaped my understanding of worth and love: if you are visible, you are vulnerable. If you are quiet, you might survive.

That little girl who ran to the door believing her father lived next door developed a terrible misconception that day: love doesn't protect, it wounds. And the rest of your life becomes a process of learning how to heal from the wounds left by those who were supposed to love you most. It would be forty years before she'd learn the truth.

# TABLE OF CONTENTS

| | |
|---|---|
| **DEDICATION** | 3 |
| **ACKNOWLEDGEMENTS** | 5 |
| **PROLOGUE** | 9 |
| CHAPTER 1: IN THE SHADOWS | 19 |
| CHAPTER 2: EXODUS FROM EGYPT | 33 |
| CHAPTER 3: FOREIGN MARRIAGE | 38 |
| CHAPTER 4: SOMEBODY ELSE'S GUY | 48 |
| CHAPTER 5: MARRIAGE REGRET | 53 |
| CHAPTER 6: JUST BE GOOD | 67 |
| CHAPTER 7: LAUNDROMAT | 76 |
| CHAPTER 8: I KNOW YOU ARE HER HUSBAND | 80 |
| CHAPTER 9: JUST GET A DIVORCE | 87 |
| CHAPTER 10: A DESPERATE YES | 94 |

| | |
|---|---:|
| CHAPTER 11: TWO LINES | 116 |
| CHAPTER 12: REVERSE DESTRUCTION | 128 |
| CHAPTER 13: WOMAN AT THE WELL | 143 |
| CHAPTER 14: STEPPING INTO THE LIGHT | 157 |
| CHAPTER 15: FINALLY HOME | 172 |
| **EPILOGUE** | **176** |
| **REFLECTION & DISCUSSION QUESTIONS** | **181** |

# CHAPTER 1

# IN THE SHADOWS

*"...and a little child will lead them." ~**Isaiah 11:6d***

Alcoholics and drug addicts raised me. This meant that I was often left to my own devices while they either slept off their high or went off in search of the next one. I never felt safe growing up.

Safety was something other children seemed to have, like warm coats in the winter or lights that stayed on when night came. For me, protection was a luxury I could never afford. From as far back as I can remember, I had to fend for myself, learning early that the world wasn't kind to little girls.

I recall nights when, at the age of three or four, I would hang on to my mother's feet and beg her not to "go out". I desperately wanted my mother to spend time cherishing and nurturing me. She would leave me with anyone, and if no one was available, she would just leave me. I remember several times waking up to find myself home alone.

It was during one of those periods of abandonment that I believe I was sexually molested at a very young age. Most of my earliest childhood memories were sexual. Once when I was roughly four, I recall while my grandmother slept off yet another drunken night, pulling down her girdle, climbing atop her naked body, and rubbing myself against her until I had an orgasm. There was another time, while my grandfather slept (also drunk), when I pulled his penis through the slit in his underwear and fondled him. I am not entirely certain, but I may have even placed it in my mouth.

I don't have a clear memory of molestation. But somehow, I knew enough to know that these actions would make my body feel a certain way. Whenever I couldn't sleep, masturbation was my go-to. I would rub my vagina against my pillow until that warm, comforting feeling would come. Somehow, deep down inside, I knew what I was doing was wrong.

Once, when I was about six, my mother caught me masturbating, instead of talking to me to find out why a six-year-old would know why or even *what* they are doing. She immediately began to whip me with a belt. Never did she ever explain human sexuality, its purpose, the dos and don'ts, or warn me about sexual predators.

I learned just how little I could rely on my mother for protection. When I was eight, something happened that should have shattered any mother's heart. I was outside, playing with two boys, when one of them decided he was going to "do it" to me (his words). He didn't penetrate, but he pressed his body against mine, ignoring my resistance, while the other boy stood by, silent. When he finally let me go, I ran home to what should've been safety. It was not.

I told my mother everything. I expected anger, outrage, protection, something, anything that would make me feel safe again. Instead, she called her friend into the room and made me repeat the story as if it were a casual anecdote. When I finished, they laughed. Laughed! She even made a crude joke about boys liking me.

My fear, my pain, my very violation, it was entertainment to her. That moment taught me that when danger came, I was on my own. As the years passed, nothing changed. When my stepfather grew angry, he often took it out on me, sometimes over things my mother did. She never defended me. She never stepped in. I was alone in every way that mattered.

***

When my baby sister was born, I slipped into the role of protector without hesitation. I was only a child myself, but something in me knew she would need someone to keep her safe.

Not long after her birth, I recall my mother leaving town for a festival with her friend and her friend's daughter, who happened to be my age.

*"Can I go?"* I asked; hope flickering inside me like a small, fragile flame.

*"No. You ain't going nowhere."* She turned to me sharply and said.

Her words slice through me like a rusty, jagged-edged knife. I watched from the window as my mother, her friend, and my friend all smiling and laughing drove away. She could have taken me. She chose not to. Instead, she left me home alone with Skeet.

Before she left, she issued a warning that still echoes in my memory: *"You better not go to Mama's house."* Her tone was ice-cold, and I understood the threat. Disobeying her meant punishment, pain I had learned not to invite. So, I stayed.

As soon as she was gone, Skeet disappeared too, probably off to drink somewhere else. The silence that settled over that house was thick and heavy, broken only by my baby sister's cries. I was nine years old, barely tall enough to reach the kitchen counter and yet, I was the only one there to care for her.

When Skeet finally stumbled back in later that evening, he was already drunk, slurring and swaying before collapsing onto the couch. He passed out cold, his snores rumbling through the house like a warning. When night fell, the baby's cries grew louder, sharper, like tiny shards of panic in the dark.

I did everything I could: rocked her, sang to her, fed her bottle after bottle but nothing worked. I tried to wake Skeet, shaking his shoulder, calling his name, even pulling at his arm. He didn't move. I might as well have been talking to the wall.

I was trapped, too scared to go to my grandparents' house and too young to know what else to do. The baby's wails pierced the quiet, and I felt so small, so helpless. Finally, with trembling hands, I picked up the phone and called my grandfather. My voice cracked as I pleaded, *"Daddy, can you please come over here and make Whitney stop crying?"*

The guilt of making that call so late, 11:30 at night weighed heavily on me. I don't know why, but I always carried a deep compassion for my grandfather; I never wanted to inconvenience him, never wanted to be a burden. But I didn't know what else to do. Through tears, I managed to choke out, *"Mama's gone, Skeet's on the couch asleep, and he won't wake up. I don't know what to do."*

Without a moment's hesitation, my grandfather got out of bed, got dressed, and drove thirty long minutes through the dark to help us.

When he arrived, he didn't scold or question me. He simply took my sister into his arms and held her close until her crying stopped. The sight of him, steady, calm, loving, was a kind of mercy I so desperately needed. For the first time that night, I felt safe. I wanted him to stay. I wanted him to take us away. But fear kept me frozen in that house. I knew I couldn't leave.

When he finally left and the house grew quiet again, I lay my sister gently in her bassinet, praying she wouldn't wake. But she did. My heart pounded as her little face scrunched up and she started to cry again. I whispered desperate promises into the dark until, at last, she drifted back to sleep.

The next morning, Skeet woke up as if none of it had happened, red-eyed and hungover, but almost cheerful. He went straight to the baby, like he'd been there all along. When I got up to help, he looked at me and said, *"What are you getting up for? I got her."*

*Yeah. Now you do.* I thought.

Later that day, my mother came home glowing from her trip, her laughter spilling through the doorway before she even set down her bags. She and her friend chattered excitedly, their voices full of warmth and joy, while my friend stood beside them, eager to share every detail. Their words were like sunlight streaming into a cold room I wasn't allowed to enter.

I stood there, trying to smile, as my friend proudly recounted everything they'd done, the rides they went on, the food they ate, and the gifts she got. She spoke to me with a kind of innocent arrogance, as if my absence had proven something that she was somehow better because her mother had taken her, because her mother loved her, and mine didn't. Each word she spoke cut deeper, her happiness becoming a mirror for my rejection.

My mother never asked how I managed, never wondered if we were okay. She didn't notice the exhaustion in my eyes or the fear I still carried from the night before. She just laughed, glowing with the joy of her weekend, completely untouched by the reality she'd left behind.

I stood there silently, invisible, watching her light up at stories that didn't include me, stories that reminded me just how forgotten I was.

\*\*\*

By the time I reached my early teens, everything that once tethered my world had fallen away. My mother had finally divorced Skeet, my grandmother had died of esophageal cancer, and not long after, my grandfather followed her, his heart giving out under the weight of his grief. Their deaths left a hollow silence in our lives. It was just the three of us now, three girls adrift in a house without rules, without guidance, without love.

With no one to hold her accountable, my mother lived however she pleased. She disappeared for entire weekends, sometimes longer, leaving me to care for my little sister. I learned to navigate the silence, to manage the fear, to pretend everything was fine. When the phone rang late at night, I'd freeze, my heart pounding, careful not to say too much. I never admitted that we were alone, never told strangers she wasn't there. I knew how dangerous the truth could be.

But my caution irritated her. *"Why do you always have to be such a smartass?"* she'd snap. *"Why can't you just answer the phone like a normal person?"*

Because I couldn't, I had to protect us because someone had to. I didn't say those words, but I felt them burning inside me. I was a child forced to live with the vigilance of an adult.

With no one watching, I had too much freedom in all the wrong ways. I recall many childhood sexual experiences. I masturbated often and had sexual intercourse for the first time when I was thirteen. When I did, I got pregnant. I had discovered sex as a tool, a way to gain the "love" I so desperately craved. Sex was an unlimited resource that I possessed that could draw almost anyone to me if only for a short period of time.

When I told my mother that I was pregnant, she didn't yell, didn't cry, didn't even look surprised. She just switched into action, like she'd been preparing for this all along. Within hours, she had an appointment scheduled. There were no questions, no "What happened?", no "Are you okay?", no "How do you feel?" She never asked why. She simply implemented a plan, cold and efficient, as though the process had already been written into our lives. One day, I was pregnant. The next day, I wasn't. And she demanded that we never speak of it again.

\*\*\*

By fourteen, even my school bus stop felt like a war zone. A boy, someone I later learned had a crush on me, tormented me every single morning. His insults were sharp and constant, and the laughter of the other kids only made it worse. No one defended me. No one told him to stop. I started standing off to the side, trying to make myself invisible. But the moment he saw me, the taunting began again, each word a reminder of how powerless I felt.

One weekend, a friend from my old school came to visit. When the same boy found out, he showed up at my house with a few others, asking to see her as if all his cruelty meant nothing, as if he had a right to cross my threshold. I told him no. I shut the door.

When my mother found out, instead of standing up for me, she turned her anger on me.

"*You're so rude,*" she hissed. "*That's why no one likes you. That's why you'll always be alone.*"

And I believed her. She made sure I did.

Between her weekend disappearances and the emotional distance that filled every day she was home, I lived in constant isolation. Even when we shared the same space, I had to call her name over and over just to get her attention. "*Mama... Mama... Mama...*" I'd repeat, my voice rising each time. She wouldn't answer until my persistence broke through her wall of indifference. And when she finally did, it was never gentle. Her tone was sharp, irritated, as if my voice was a sound she despised.

"*What?!*" she snapped.

No matter what I asked, whether I wanted to show her something, ask a question, or just talk, her response was always the same: "*I don't care. Get out of my face.*"

I learned the shape of rejection not as a single moment, but as a rhythm. The silence. The indifference. The casual cruelty. I stopped expecting to be heard. I stopped trying to be seen.

A year and a half after my grandfather died, we moved to Tennessee. My mother said it was to be closer to family, but for me, it felt like stepping into a wider circle of rejection. Because she'd had me so young, some of her first cousins were actually younger than me. While they were my blood, I had no place among them– not because of age, but because my mother, the oldest of the first cousins, wanted the freedom to be with her peers, her cousins.

The first weekend we were there, the cousins made plans to go bowling. I watched from the driveway as they piled into cars, laughing and shouting each other's names. I longed to go with them, to belong, to feel like maybe, just maybe, I could be a part of something that felt normal. But my mother didn't hesitate. She was the oldest cousin, and she wanted her time with her peers, the ones she had grown up with, without me tagging along.

*"You're staying here,"* she said, blocking the doorway as if I'd even thought to argue. *"You're not a first cousin."*

So, I stayed at home with my then five-year-old sister and my great-grandfather, feeling the weight of her words settle over me like a heavy coat. Outside, the older cousins laughed, building memories I would never share with them. Inside, I continued the lesson of existing in the shadows of my mother's choices.

That rejection wasn't accidental. It was deliberate. My mother made sure I was isolated in everyone's eyes, not just mine. She told my cousins lies about me, shaping their perception before I even had a chance to know them.

All they knew about me was what she told them: that I was spoiled, that I got everything I wanted, that I didn't listen, and that I was hard to deal with. I didn't know any of it at the time.

It took years for the truth to trickle out, years until one cousin, tired of believing the lies, finally confessed. She shared that once, when my mother needed to borrow money, as she often did without repayment, she told that cousin that I was living with her and refusing to pay bills. A complete fabrication meant to shame me and justify her request.

This happened so often, so consistently, that by the time I became an adult, the damage had already been done. Many still chose to believe her stories, even after she was gone. My sister and I still feel the sting of it, still mistreated by people who should have been our family, all because of the lies my mother planted.

She always made sure I knew I was unwanted, not just with whispers, but with words sharp enough to cut. I could never forget the frequent bursts of rage:

*"I hate you. I wish you were never born!"*

Those words echoed long after they were said. They built walls, walls between me and the family I should have belonged to, walls between me and the world that made sense for everyone else but me.

So, it was no surprise that by the time I was in high school, when I told my mother that one of her male friends had molested me, she barely reacted. The truth was, there were two men, both of her friends, both of whom she had living with us at the time.

Her response? For the first man, she claimed she spoke to him about it, or maybe she didn't. I'll never know. What I do know is that she came back to me later and said, almost casually, *"Fred said he's not going to bother you anymore."*

As if that was supposed to make everything okay. As if those words could erase what had happened.

The second time it happened, she didn't even bother pretending to care. I found out from a neighbor–*a neighbor*– that my mother had told her that I was *"just seeking attention."* Those words gutted me. To her, my pain was an inconvenience, my trauma an exaggeration.

Not long after that, she and Skeet remarried. Surprisingly, she asked for my opinion as if my thoughts suddenly mattered. *"What do you think about me marrying Skeet again?"* she asked. She was excited, like something had changed.

I remember answering in the calmest voice, my tone was flat, emotionless: *"I don't care. I'm older now, and I don't have to take his crap."*

Her reply was immediate, almost rehearsed: *"You're still a child, and he's an adult. You have to respect him."*

I didn't say a word. I just walked away. I didn't know how it was going to play out, but I meant what I said. At that point, nothing she said or did mattered anymore. Skeet was just another person added to the long list of people who could treat me any kind of way. She must've told him because he didn't put his hands on me anymore, but that didn't stop his words from cutting.

One day, when I was sixteen, he got angry over something so trivial, I don't remember what, probably because I was still in my pajamas late in the day. He sneered, *"You need to carry yourself in a respectable way."* Respectable?! Really?!

These people lecturing me about respect were the same ones who had me lying on the phone to their friends' mothers just to get money for drugs. The same ones who had me committing credit card fraud, putting checks in my name when I had no account. The same ones who left me scrubbing blood splatters off the bathroom walls after their friends came over and used it as a shooting gallery. Respect?! From them?!

The word itself was a joke. I had no respect for them. How could I? And worse, I had none left for myself. His tone dripped with disgust, like I was the problem, like I was the stain on their lives. Then, without hesitation, he said something that made my stomach twist, my chest tighten, and for a split second, I wanted to throw up. He said, *"Even Carl (one of their drug friends) wants to f--- you. The only reason he doesn't is because of the respect he has for your mother."* There's that word again.

I remember standing there, feeling hollow, like all the air had been sucked out of the room. I was sixteen years old. A child. Somehow, I was the one blamed, the one shamed, the one made to feel dirty.

I wanted to call the police. I wanted someone to come and shatter the chaos that passed for a home. I used to imagine detectives coming in to see the blood splatters on the walls and the drug paraphernalia in the garbage, to end the madness that had become my normal. But fear always silenced me. I was terrified that if I called, nothing would change because nothing ever did. And worse, that I'd be punished for daring to ask for help. Maybe blamed. Maybe beaten.

So instead, I sought refuge wherever I could find it. I began spending more time at a neighbor's house, a beautiful lady who lived across the street, named Ms. Ann. Her home became my safe haven; the place I secretly called home until I graduated high school and left for basic training.

## CHAPTER 2

# EXODUS FROM EGYPT

*"Forget the former things; do not dwell on the past."*
*~Isaiah 43:18*

My military career was in jeopardy before it even started.

It was my mother who planted the idea of joining the military. I joined the Army Delayed Entry Program (DEP) at 17, just one week after my birthday. I'll never forget September 23, 1983, the day I visited the Military Entrance Processing Station, underwent a physical examination, selected a job, and signed my contract. Three weeks into my senior year of high school, I was officially in the DEP as a 75C Personnel Management Specialist. I was ready for my ship date on June 19, 1984.

However, trouble had already found me. In November 1982, at the age of 16, I was arrested because I was hanging out with the wrong people. The wrong people were Mama and Skeet.

About a week before Thanksgiving, Skeet and I went downtown to Harvey's department store. In his possession, he had a fraudulent credit card. He and my mother had a scheme where they would apply for credit cards under assumed identities, using our home address. One such card arrived just before Christmas. My mother had broken her ankle the week before our "shopping" trip, so she couldn't go with him. Instead, she sent me.

We took the city bus downtown, and it wasn't until Skeet told me to pick out anything I wanted that I began to realize something wasn't right. That had never happened before. After making my selections, we went upstairs to buy traveler's checks using the fraudulent credit card. They planned to use the card to buy traveler's checks and then destroy it. As we were checking out, Skeet abruptly said, *"Let's go!"*

*"But what about the stuff I want?"* I asked, confused.

He insisted we leave immediately. At the bus stop, just as the bus arrived, two men in suits approached us, flashed their badges, and escorted us back inside. They led us to an office and left us alone. Skeet turned to me and said, *"If they ask, my name is Monty Cavern."*

I was terrified. I feared that if I told the truth, he'd escape punishment as always, and I'd be the one to suffer. So, I lied.

Whenever I protested my mother and Skeet's criminal activities, she would accuse me of thinking I was better than them, of talking too much, of being a "goody two-shoes." Also, Skeet had beaten my mother, my siblings, and me countless times, yet he never seemed to face real consequences. So, I stuck to the lie until I was alone in the police car on my way to juvenile detention.

The officer told me that if I told the truth, I could go home that night. That was all I needed to hear. Like the chubby kid in Steven Spielberg's *The Goonies*, I spilled everything, names, dates, Social Security numbers, all of it. If I knew it, I told it.

True to his word, they called my mother and told her to come get me. But because of her broken ankle, she sent Carl, of all people, instead. The booking officer refused to release me to anyone but her. I had to wait until she finally showed up at midnight. I had school the next day.

I was charged with conspiracy to commit fraud. My trial took place a year later, after I had already joined the DEP. The officer who had encouraged me to confess was no longer on the force and couldn't testify on my behalf. My mother sat in the courtroom, silent, offering no defense for me. But my public defender used my enlistment in the Army to appeal to the judge. I was convicted but received only six months of unsupervised probation, which ended just before my high school graduation.

Then, in January 1984, I almost got arrested *again*.

During another one of his drunken rages, Skeet attacked my mother again. This time, I decided I wasn't going to take it anymore. I stood in the dark with a meat cleaver, ready to strike as he passed. But something, which I now recognize as the Holy Spirit, stopped me. I hesitated, weighing my options. I put the cleaver away. But the fight escalated. Skeet grabbed a lead pipe and attacked us. I wrestled it from him and ran outside, only to find the police waiting.

Relieved, I broke down in tears. But Skeet kept yelling and cursing. When he lifted his hand and pointed at my mother's face, she began to scream. In the chaos, I had grabbed a knife, and before any of us fully realized what had happened, I had severed his left index finger. When he raised his hand, it was hanging by the skin. The police immediately put me in handcuffs.

Thankfully, this was still a time when officers asked victims if they wanted to press charges against the perpetrator. Skeet declined. My mother, finally finding her voice, told them I was only defending her. They removed the handcuffs, and I couldn't stop crying. In a strange way, I felt both relief and grief, relief because I thought it was finally over, that maybe this nightmare would end; grief because I was utterly exhausted. I was tired of staying up every weekend to keep him from killing her, tired of trying to protect my sister, who, ironically, had slept through the chaos. I just wanted peace. I wanted him gone.

But he wasn't. They took him to the hospital, and when he was released, my mother let him come back. When I protested, she sent me to live with someone else.

I was beyond ready to leave.

On June 19, 1984, just two weeks after graduating from high school, I left for basic training. I call that day my *Exodus from Egypt*. Finally, I was free from the judgment and abuse I had endured for so long. Finally, I could build a life filled with love and acceptance.

Or so I thought.

I had left *Egypt*, but *Egypt* was still in me. I had no idea how to live the life I longed for. Instead of healing, I carried the poison they had infused into my soul and spread it to everyone I encountered, starting with Terrance.

# CHAPTER 3

# FOREIGN MARRIAGE

*"You, my brothers and sisters, were called to be free. But do not use your freedom to indulge the flesh; rather, serve one another humbly in love."* **~Galatians 5:13**

I knew the night before that I didn't want to marry him. But we were in Odense, Denmark. I was 18 years old, in a place I never dreamed I would be. How many girls could say, "I got married in Denmark," aside from those who lived there or in a neighboring country? Not some poor Black girl from Nashville, and certainly not one whom everyone had constantly reminded that no one would ever want her.

"*I'll show them,*" I thought. Not only did someone want me, but we were getting married in Denmark.

Terrance and I were six months into an eighteen-month overseas assignment. Fresh out of Advanced Individual Training (AIT) Rhein-Main Air Base in Frankfurt, Germany, was our first duty station as Army junior enlisted soldiers. I figured it wasn't a big deal.

"*We'll just get divorced when we return to the States,*" I thought. I had no idea he was serious. After all, the whole thing was my idea.

Terrance was kind and quiet. He was responsible and followed the rules. I would see him come and go in the barracks, but I paid him little attention. My focus was on the rowdier group, those who held regular happy hours in their rooms during the week and hung out in the cadre barracks on the weekends.

They were the more seasoned soldiers in the unit. I was captivated by the sense of community they seemed to share. I wanted to be part of it. They called me "Baby Girl" because I was just three months past my eighteenth birthday when I arrived.

Every day after work, I'd go to the dining facility for dinner, then rush back to my room to change before heading to whatever room was the designated hangout for the night. Some soldiers were cooks who had to be up by three or four in the morning, so they would get off work and start the parties early. If I wasn't in one room, I was in another, anywhere but alone. I hated being alone. Having been left to my own devices as a child, and being in a foreign country less than a year out of high school only intensified my desire for companionship.

One evening, instead of following my usual routine, I decided to check out the beer tent, a makeshift bar inside a large circus tent since the junior enlisted club was under renovation. Terrance was at the bar eating a chili dog and drinking a soda. I joined him, and we spent hours talking. We discovered we were both from Tennessee, and he had been one class behind me in AIT. We shared similar interests, particularly in board games like Scrabble and music. He was funny. From that night on, we were inseparable.

Most military installations have a tour and travel office where personnel can book recreational trips and tours. At the front of the office, a rack held fliers advertising trips to various destinations. That's where I saw it, a marriage train to Denmark. *"Is this what I think it is?"* I asked the clerk. He explained that the trip was designed for people who wanted a hassle-free wedding ceremony. I shared this with Terrance, indirectly proposing to him. "We should get married," I said, as if it were just something to do on a Saturday.

In June 1985, Terrance and I boarded a train for Denmark. It was incredible. The train was open, clean, and bright, just as it was in the travel catalogs. We played Scrabble on the table between us and took in the beautiful European countryside. It felt like a fairytale.

I was young, naive, and broken, traveling from country to country like I owned everything. Upon arrival in Odense, we ate at McDonald's because we didn't have much money and because I had a tradition of eating at McDonald's in every country I visited. We walked in the park and went canoeing, though that turned out to be more work than fun. The next day, we went to the city courthouse and got married.

Terrance and I could have had a good marriage. We were two young people just starting adult life. Two poor kids who understood the struggles of barely having enough food, a warm place to sleep, and the need for safety and protection.

Raised by single parents in the ghetto, we knew what it was like to miss out on activities because of a lack of money.

We shared the same general vision for the future. The problem was that we never actually discussed it, and there was a major difference between us that we had not acknowledged. Terrance was raised as a Christian. His mother instilled faith in him. If he knew anything, he knew he loved God and wanted to serve Him. I, on the other hand, wasn't thinking about Jesus and nobody else. I was focused on myself.

When Terrance and I returned, we tried to settle into some kind of normal life as a couple. Still, trouble seemed to cling to me like a shadow I couldn't shake. I had recently faced punishment under the Uniform Code of Military Justice (UCMJ), reduced in rank from Private E2 to Private E1 after receiving an Article 15 for fighting in the barracks, showing up late or hungover to work, and a host of other poor decisions. When I was with Terrance, I felt a flicker of hope that maybe I could become more grounded, more disciplined, maybe even better. But the world, and especially this unit, wasn't as forgiving. The weight of my mistakes, the stigma that followed me, made it hard to move forward, no matter how much I wanted to.

To give me a fresh start, my supervisor recommended that I be reassigned to another unit located north of Frankfurt, in the small city of Garlstedt. Through it all, Terrance was patient and kind, steady in a way I didn't know I needed. He never raised his voice or met my chaos with anger; instead, he met it with grace. When the decision to reassign me was made, he agreed to go with me. We arrived as husband and wife, ready to build our life together. We moved into an off-base apartment, bought a small car, and for a moment, everything felt perfect, until I got acclimated.

***

Michael was tall, funny, and confident. Like me, he was married, but that didn't matter to either of us. Especially not to me because he wanted me. Having been denied my whole life, being desired was my aphrodisiac. I don't know how it started, but before long, Michael and I were a couple, and everyone knew it, even our spouses. Michael's wife was passive, almost mousy. It was like she was used to his behavior. Terrance carried himself as though he were completely unaware. But he knew. If for no other reason than everyone else knew. I remember the stares and the shaking of the heads, and my first sergeant, who practically despised me and my blatant disrespect for the marital institution. Through it all, Terrance maintained his dignity.

Michael and I spent every stolen moment together, craving each other's presence wherever we could find it. We would sit in the car for hours, lingering in silence or whispered conversation, steal lunches during the workday, and escape at every chance we had. It didn't matter where we were; just being near him felt like everything.

One night, while his wife was at work, we crossed a line that made the thrill and the fear impossible to ignore.

"Spend the night with me?" he'd asked earlier that day. "Tamara has guard duty. She won't be home until morning."

He didn't have to ask me twice.

Later that evening, I lied and told Terrance that I had duty as well. My heart pounded as I changed clothes in my car, the weight of deception pressing hard against my chest. When I entered Michael's house, everything about it whispered of a shared life: the framed photos, the matching towels, the gentle scent of her perfume still lingering in the air. It was a home, their home. And yet, there I was.

A sickness stirred deep in my stomach, but my feelings for Michael drowned out every warning, logic, morals, and even self-respect. All of it faded beneath the intoxication of wanting to be wanted. As he led me to the bedroom, my mind screamed, "Girl, what are you doing? You're not even going to enjoy this." But selfishness won. I silenced my conscience and followed him into her bed.

We drifted off, tangled in the warmth of our recklessness, until the sound of furious banging shattered the night.

Tamara had come home early. Her key wouldn't turn because he had double-bolted the door, his own key still in the lock. Panic ripped through me. My eyes flew open, heart slamming in my chest. I snatched up my clothes, too terrified to dress, and bolted for the balcony.

The cold night air hit me like a slap as I climbed over the railing, whispering a desperate prayer under my breath. Thank God they lived on the first floor.

The bushes broke my fall, though the branches tore at my skin, leaving angry scratches along my arms and legs. I scrambled to my feet, dressing right there in the dirt, trembling as twigs clung to my hair and clothes. My breath came in ragged gasps, part shame, part terror.

When I finally made it to my car, I slammed the door shut and sat there shaking, barely dressed, heart hammering against my ribs. The silence inside the car was deafening. A rush of exhilaration, guilt, and horror collided inside me, leaving me hollow.

That night, as I drove away into the darkness, I knew something inside me had changed. I had crossed a line I could never uncross.

The recklessness continued for months, until the last straw came one Saturday after a night of dancing. Michael and I stayed in a hotel, caught up in our secret world. It felt beautiful, fleeting, until I got home the next morning. Terrance was waiting, furious. Something in him broke; he had taken all the disrespect he was going to take, so he locked all my clothing, except for my military uniforms, in the basement.

He stripped me out of my clothes and told me I wasn't to leave the house except for work and only in uniform.

"Who do you think you are? You can't tell me what to do!" I screamed.

He locked me in the bedroom that had a balcony. "You'll stay in there until it's time to go to work," he said.

What he didn't realize was that I had no shame, and he had completely forgotten about the balcony. Dressed only in my bra and panties, I climbed over the third-floor balcony onto my neighbors' below. They immediately called the military police. By the time they arrived, my neighbor had covered me with a blanket, trying to offer some semblance of dignity.

When the officers spoke to me, they asked what had happened. I explained that I had stayed out all night and didn't see the big deal. I told them, plainly, that I didn't want to be married anymore, as if ending a marriage were something you could undo on a Saturday.

Shortly after, Terrance and I separated and moved to the barracks. I wanted nothing more to do with him or our marriage. Still, he desperately tried to hold on. He had been raised to understand the sacred value of marriage, the importance of honoring God in a relationship, and the work it takes to build a home and a life together. My heart breaks for him because he did everything he knew to save us. He went to therapy. He begged me to go with him. I initially refused. When I did go, I went in defiance, only to leave abruptly when the conversation turned towards salvaging the relationship.

To me, our vows were empty words, spoken hastily and without any real meaning. My mother had taught me that if it didn't work out, I could always get a divorce. A notion I carried like a hidden weapon, ready to use whenever I no longer wanted to continue. Terrance didn't know, couldn't know, that I had already made up my mind long before we ever said, "I do."

Michael ended our relationship to stay with his wife, leaving me alone in the wreckage of the mess we had made. Still legally married, I stumbled through two more volatile relationships after moving into the barracks, grasping at fleeting connections to fill a deep and aching emptiness inside me. It was during the latter of those relationships that I became pregnant with my daughter.

During my pregnancy, Terrance, having received a hardship reassignment, mailed me divorce papers. I signed and returned them, numb and stoic. Just like that, with the stroke of a pen, my *first* marriage was over.

My daughter's father was never truly committed to me. I'll never forget the day I overheard him on the phone with his mother and aunt. When they learned I was pregnant, their words cut deep. His mother practically slapped me across the face with her judgment:

*"What kind of girl joins the Army and gets pregnant by someone else's boyfriend? I thought young women joined the military to go to college!"*

He stood there in silence, offering no defense, no reassurance, nothing. He was almost smiling. That's when I learned that his high school sweetheart had been waiting for him to come home from Germany all along. I felt like a complete fool.

My daughter was born in Bremerhaven, Germany, on October 5, 1987. In early December, I returned with her to the

United States, alone. Her father made it clear that everything that happened in Germany would stay in Germany. Even though she bore his name, he had signed the birth certificate, he dismissed his responsibility. Since he wasn't in the United States, I couldn't sue him for child support. So, I moved on and left the past behind.

## CHAPTER 4

# SOMEBODY ELSE'S GUY

*"But for those who are self-seeking and who reject the truth and follow evil, there will be wrath and anger."*
*~Romans 2:8*

When I was in high school, I longed for the kind of relationship where a boy and a girl would walk through the halls together, him carrying her books, waiting outside her classroom, and walking her to her next class. Of course, that wasn't very practical; he would have to leave his class early to be there when hers ended, and then arrive late to his own after escorting her. But when you're in high school and selfish, you don't think about logistics; you just know what you want.

I observed a similar dynamic unfold with one particular couple. The guy's name was Kenneth. I would always see him walking his girlfriend to class, and I thought they were so special. I wanted that. Eventually, Kenneth and his girlfriend broke up, and I started dating him. It was a wonderful relationship. He introduced me to his family, took me to his house for dinner, and they even picked me up for church. For the first time, I felt like I belonged to him, to them, to something bigger than myself.

Kenneth had always talked about joining the military. His grandfather had served, and for as long as he could remember, that was his dream. I, on the other hand, just wanted to get away from where we were, and he promised he would take me with him. But that was just childhood talk. We got into a huge fight and eventually broke up.

At the time, I was in the 11th grade. By my senior year, I had transferred to a different school and joined the DEP. After graduation, just before I was set to leave for basic training, I ran into Kenneth at a gas station. He told me that he had also enlisted in the Army and would be heading to basic training soon. I thought that would be the last time I saw him. I was wrong.

\*\*\*

When I arrived at Rhein-Main Air Base in Frankfurt, Germany, actually, that was just the reception station, the place where newly arrived soldiers were processed before being assigned to their permanent units. I sat there anxiously, waiting to find out where I would be stationed, feeling both nervous and alone in a foreign country for the first time.

As I sat there, lost in thought, I suddenly saw a familiar face. Kenneth, along with another soldier, walked up the steps. They were there to pick up some new soldiers for their unit. The moment I saw him, relief washed over me. Without thinking, I jumped up and ran to him, wrapping my arms around him in a tight hug, an act that was strictly forbidden while in uniform. But in that moment, I didn't care. I was overwhelmed, homesick, and desperate for anything familiar.

Kenneth and I kept in touch after that, talking occasionally whenever we had the chance. When he found out I was about to marry Terrance, he came to see me. We went out to a club, had some drinks, and danced, reminiscing about old times. Then, in the middle of it all, he asked no, begged me not to marry Terrance. My mind was already made up. Realizing there was nothing he could do, he left that night, defeated. Once again, I thought it would be the last time I ever saw him. Again, I was wrong.

***

Two years into my overseas tour in Germany and estranged from Terrance, I took thirty days of leave and returned home to Nashville. I didn't tell anyone I was coming. The city felt both familiar and alien, like a memory that had been layered over a lifetime of absence.

It was a warm summer day when I landed after a grueling nine-hour flight from Frankfurt. I took a taxi to my mother's last known address, the house she had just bought before I left. But when we arrived, the place was empty. My mother was gone. My sister was gone. I didn't know where either of them was. I immediately felt a hollow ache of disorientation and uncertainty.

I knew her neighbors, and I knocked on their door. They were thrilled to see me and shared what they knew. My mother had divorced Skeet, again, left the house, and was now living in an apartment, though they didn't know the address. But God was with me, because it turned out to be the same complex we had lived in when we first moved to Nashville years ago.

I returned to the waiting taxi and had him drive me to the apartments that I remember from my initial arrival in Nashville. As we approached, I noticed children playing in the park, splashing in the pool. Then I saw her, my ten-year-old sister, in the water. Her eyes locked on me, and she leapt out, calling, "Sisty!" She ran into my arms, and for a fleeting moment, the chaos of the world outside melted away. I felt a surge of relief and love, of finally being home.

But that feeling shattered the moment we reached my mother's apartment. She screamed at the top of her lungs, claiming she had seen a ghost. "You're supposed to be in Germany!" she shouted.

She was right. I *was* supposed to be in Germany, but I had come back to surprise her, to reconnect, to find something real in the pieces of our fractured lives. I had expected happiness, perhaps even warmth. I had hoped that after drug rehab and a couple of years of recovery, she had changed. But she hadn't. Not at all. The homecoming I had imagined, the one I had longed for during lonely nights abroad, turned into a confrontation with a past I could neither outrun nor fix.

While in Nashville, I ran into Kenneth yet again. Seeing him was like stepping back in time, a rush of old emotions surfacing before I could stop them. He looked the same, but his life had taken a turn I hadn't expected. He had been involuntarily discharged from the military and was now engaged to be married. That fact should have been enough to keep me away, but it didn't.

Despite everything, we fell back into something that felt like a relationship. Whether I believed, deep down, that he might leave her for me, or if I was just clinging to the comfort of the familiar, I don't know. Maybe I just didn't want to face how wrong it was. Whatever my expectations were, they were misguided on every level. The situation was doomed from the start, and when it ended, it ended badly.

One night, while I was sitting at home watching television alone, Kenneth knocked on my door and called me outside. There was something in his voice, something urgent, and without thinking, I went. When I reached his car, my heart sank. His fiancée was sitting in the front seat. He motioned me over, and as I stood there, vulnerable under the harsh glow of the streetlights, he looked me in the eye and said, *"I do not want to be with you. I am going to marry her."*

The embarrassment, the humiliation, the sharp sting of rejection, I can't even put into words. I stood there, frozen, as the weight of it settled in, as reality crashed down around me. I had made a mistake, a terrible mistake, and I had no choice but to face it. I went back to my apartment defeated, certain this would be the last time I ever saw him. Again, I was wrong. But the next time would be my own undoing.

## CHAPTER 5

# MARRIAGE REGRET

*"Wives, in the same way submit yourselves to your own husbands." ~1 Peter 3:1a*

Ellis said it with such conviction: *"I'm gon' marry Mayes."*

He believed it with all his heart. But I did everything in my power to prove him wrong. I didn't want to marry him. He was dorky, skinny, sweet, and innocent. He was the kind of man who would treat me well, who would love me fully and unconditionally.

Like me, he had suffered a childhood void of love and affection. But I wasn't looking for that. I wanted someone hard, rough around the edges. I craved excitement, danger, the type of love that came with bruises and battles. I wanted ghetto, hood, and to be disrespected. I didn't recognize the treasure he was, the diamond in the rough. To this day, letting him go remains my greatest regret.

In January 1988, I arrived in El Paso, Texas, reassigned from Germany with my three-month-old baby, ready to begin a new chapter. After securing an apartment and arranging childcare, I started working in the officer records department.

That was where I met Ellis. He worked in the section next door, and every chance he got, whenever his supervisor wasn't watching, he was at my desk, talking to me, smiling, making me laugh. He had a quiet persistence about him, a patience that I didn't appreciate at the time. I barely noticed him, too caught up chasing after men I found more exciting, more enticing. But in the end, Ellis was the only one who showed me genuine love.

He was determined. On Valentine's Day, I arrived at work to find an envelope waiting on my desk, a dinner invitation. But this wasn't just *any* dinner invitation. This one was carefully planned, handwritten with details about what to wear, what time to be ready, and a sweet reassurance not to worry about childcare because *everything* had already been taken care of.

I was thrilled. The rest of the day, I floated through work in a haze of excitement and disbelief, smiling at the thought that someone had gone to such lengths just to make me feel special. A friend of ours, who happened to work in the same office, walked past my desk, and I couldn't hold it in.

"Girl, look at this!" I said, waving the invitation like it was a golden ticket.

She laughed knowingly and said, "I know," her grin giving her away. She was the babysitter! She had helped him plan every last detail. That only made it sweeter.

I couldn't focus on anything but the evening ahead. When I got home, I bathed my baby, fed her, tucked her in with kisses, and made sure everything was perfect before turning my attention to myself. I took my time getting dressed, feeling butterflies flutter in my stomach like I hadn't felt in years.

When Ellis arrived, he looked at me with that soft, admiring smile that said everything without a word. The dinner reservations were for Benihana's. That was the first time I had ever been there, or to any restaurant quite like it. The sounds, the aroma, the lively energy, all felt new and enchanting. It wasn't about the restaurant, though; it was about *him*, the care, the thoughtfulness, the way he made me feel seen. Aside from a high school boyfriend who once took me to dinner, this was the first time, as an adult, that I had been treated with such tenderness and intention.

Ellis told me about his childhood as if it belonged to someone else, like he was still trying to convince himself it had really happened. He grew up on a farm, raised by his grandparents, people who believed that work was the only kind of love worth showing. There were no Christmas mornings with presents under a tree, no birthday parties, no cards or cake or laughter. Just another dawn, another task, another reminder that he existed to labor, not to be loved.

From the time he was old enough to stand on his own, he was expected to pull his weight. Feeding animals, mending fences, hauling heavy buckets through the heat of summer. He said he hated summer because there was no escape, no school, no rest, just work until his body ached and his spirit dulled.

School was his only safe place. He said it was the one part of his life that made sense. He was good at math, brilliant, even. Numbers were honest, predictable, and fair. Two plus two always equaled four, no matter who you were or how much love you didn't get. It gave him a kind of control he never had at home. But at the end of the day, he still had to go back to that house where affection was rationed like water in a drought. His grandparents also raised his cousin, and that cousin was the golden one, the one who got the new clothes, the kind words, the small mercies. He was the black sheep, the one they tolerated but never treasured. He learned early that love was something other people received, and that gifts, celebrations, even simple care, were luxuries he would never know.

So when he grew up, he didn't know how to give love in the ways most people expected. He didn't know what gifts were supposed to mean because he had never been given any. And when he did try, when he offered me something simple or practical instead of what I had hinted at, I took it as a personal insult.

I didn't see the effort behind it. I saw only the lack. Instead of grace, I gave him grief. Instead of understanding, I turned it into another argument. I'd throw it in his face, accusing him of not caring, not paying attention, not loving me the way I wanted to be loved. Each time, he'd withdraw a little more, and I'd push a little harder, until it turned into yet another shouting match, another put-down, another humiliation.

He had trusted me with his story, his pain, and I used it as ammunition. When I met Ellis, he didn't have much. He lived in the barracks and didn't own a car. I, on the other hand, had a daughter to care for, which meant I needed stability, a home, transportation, and a routine. My car was my lifeline: daycare drop-offs, doctor's appointments, work shifts, everything. I even used that as a weapon. Once, while driving together, we got into an argument over something trivial. I remember pulling over, throwing harsh words at him, and ordering him out of my car like I was cutting him out of my life.

When I was angry, I wanted to hurt him where he was weakest, and I did. I'd remind him of everything he wasn't given, everything he never had, as if his deprivation was his fault. I bullied him with his own past, thinking that breaking him down would somehow make him fight for me, prove that he loved me. One night, I went too far. My words were cruel, deliberate, meant to sting. He tried to walk away, but I wouldn't let him. I followed him, shouting, demanding something, anything, that felt like passion. When he finally turned and grabbed me by the neck, his hand was shaking. I could tell he was fighting the urge to strike me, fighting to control himself. But I wouldn't stop. I mistook that tension, that chaos, for love.

Back then, I thought love had to hurt to be real. I thought pain was proof of passion. Now I see that what we called love was really survival, two broken people reenacting old wounds, hoping to find healing in each other's scars.

He didn't know how to give gifts, and I didn't know how to receive grace. He trusted me with the truth, and I used it to wound him. That's the part that still stings, the knowing that I became what had always hurt him most.

I see now that he truly loved me. He was patient with me, enduring my reckless antics and self-sabotage. He adopted my daughter, the child I had given birth to in Germany after her father abandoned her.

That kind of love was rare. It was the kind of love I should have held onto. But I was foolish. I wasn't settled in my spirit. It wasn't enough for me. I was always searching, always restless, trying to fill a void that I didn't yet understand.

I was reckless with his heart. I broke up with him one day and went back the next, over and over again. I cheated on him with his friend and coworker, and then had the audacity to be angry when he lied to me about going out with his friends. Looking back, I see how I pushed him away, yet he never truly retreated. He remained steadfast, wanting to stay married to me no matter what.

All Ellis ever wanted was to be loved, to build the family he never had as a child, and all I did was hurt him because of my own brokenness. During one of our infamous "off-again" seasons, when love felt more like tug-of-war than covenant, he volunteered for an overseas tour in Korea. I didn't know about it until the orders came down official, stamped, and real.

By the time I learned of it, we were back "on again," tangled in that familiar cycle of breaking apart and running back together. We were married, and this time the stakes were different. His reasoning? He said he wanted to escape the heartache I kept inflicting on him every breakup, every tear, every slammed door. Signing up for Korea was, in his mind, a way to get distance from me. But because we were married, distance was the last thing I wanted. So, I did what any stubborn, prideful, young wife would do. I requested Korea, too. I left my daughter with my mother, packed my uniforms, and followed him across the world.

Korea was a shock to my system. A sharp, unkind jolt. I hated every minute of it, the damp, bitter cold in the winter, the thick humidity in the summer, even the strange smells that hung in the air like something foreign and unwelcome. Nothing about it felt like home. To make matters worse, we didn't even get to live together.

Lower-enlisted soldiers weren't granted that privilege. He had a bunk in one building with a roommate. I had a room in another building with my own roommate. We were in the same country, the same post, but still worlds apart. It was in Korea that I got pregnant with my second daughter. I say "mine" and not "ours" because the truth is, today, I don't know if he was the father.

I was promiscuous. Reckless. I cheated constantly. My body was there in Korea, but my heart, my faithfulness, and my sense of self-control were scattered in a thousand directions.

Pregnancy, though, has a way of forcing decisions. Because I couldn't fly after a certain number of months, the Army sent me home two months early. Korea was supposed to be a one-year tour. I only lasted ten months. Once I got home, he followed a week later on leave. When I gave birth, he was granted an early return, which meant he never had to go back to Korea. On March 28, 1990, in Highland Park, Illinois, I delivered my second daughter. She arrived in the world carrying all the questions, all the chaos, and all the unfinished business of our marriage.

Yet, it wasn't all bad. We had fun together. Ellis loved video games. Because he never had toys as a child, as an adult, he immersed himself in games and music. He'd ask me to be his quarterback when he played football on the console, and at the time, I'd roll my eyes, thinking it was silly. Now, I look back on those moments with a smile. They were small, ordinary, but they were ours.

The way he treated my oldest daughter melted me. He'd play rap music loud enough to shake the windows, and she'd dance and twirl around the living room, her laughter mixing with the beat. Once during their play, she said, "Give me some lips, Daddy!" But when he tried to kiss her, she cried out, "No lips!" and pointed to the ChapStick instead. We later realized "lips" was her word for ChapStick, and it became their little inside joke. One that still makes me smile whenever I think about it.

Sometimes I'd come home ready to fuss about the noise, but then I'd see her lying on the floor in front of the speaker, sound asleep, the music still blasting. He'd be nearby, playing his video game or just keeping watch over her, two peas in a pod, perfectly at peace. For all the chaos between us, I couldn't have been more grateful for how he loved her in those moments.

But I could never find peace. Angry outbursts became commonplace, and nothing ever seemed to satisfy me. Both Ellis and I had grown up in emotionally and spiritually unhealthy environments, so we tried to create something better for the people we loved. We brought our siblings to live with us, hoping to give them a sense of stability in a home that was clean, calm, and safe. We wanted them to have opportunities we never did. His mother had also been a single parent struggling to make ends meet, and deep down, I was always worried that my sister, like me, was unprotected.

One summer, Ellis's younger brother, who was the same age as my sister, came to stay with us. At first, I told myself that I was just frustrated because he and Ellis spent so much time together, playing video games, laughing, and bonding. But the truth is, it wasn't jealousy, it was anger. He became an outlet for the rage I didn't understand, the anger that had nowhere else to go. I picked at him constantly.

"Clean this up," "Do that," "Why haven't you finished?" He was only fifteen; just a boy far from home, and our house was a world away from what he was used to. We both worked, we had two little girls, and I tried desperately to keep everything in order.

One day, during another one of my tirades, I was yelling at him again. Ellis finally snapped. He grabbed me, held me tightly, and shouted, "Stop! Leave him alone!" But my pride and ego couldn't take it. In that instant, I felt humiliated, disrespected, and exposed. My mind screamed, *Oh no he didn't. How dare he embarrass me in front of his brother?*

Rage flooded through me, hot and uncontrollable. I wanted to fight him. I wanted to fight them both. I just wanted to release everything building inside of me, years of anger, pain, and resentment.

When he finally let me go, I knew right then: if I swung on either of them, they might team up on me for real. So instead, I turned that fury loose on everything around me. I became a storm, a tornado tearing through the house. I started in the kitchen, throwing open cabinets and hurling their contents to the floor. Plates shattered, spices scattered, and my screams filled the air. I don't even remember what I said, only the sound of my own voice, raw and breaking.

The shame, the anger, was too much. Years of buried emotion poured out all at once. I was crying, yelling, destroying, and suddenly I realized I was losing control of my body. I felt the warmth of urine running down my legs, but even then, a voice inside whispered, *You're peeing on yourself.* And another voice, louder, defiant answered, *If I stop, I'll have to calm down. And I don't want to calm down.*

It was a war between my mind and my rage, and I was losing. I didn't stop until my strength was gone. When the fury finally drained from me, I collapsed in the middle of the floor, sobbing. My pants were soaked, my heart was broken, and I was consumed with humiliation. I could hear Ellis in the background, his voice frantic, telling his brother to call the police. My babies, just one and three years old, were crying, terrified.

Thank God they didn't make that call. When the storm passed, I dragged myself to the bathroom, stripped off my wet clothes, and stood under the shower, letting the water wash away what I couldn't put into words. Then I went to bed empty, ashamed, and exhausted. The weight of what had just happened pressed down on me so heavily that I could hardly breathe.

And still... Ellis stayed.

One of my biggest issues in our marriage was my obsession with how others perceived me. I struggled with insecurity and allowed outward appearances to influence how I viewed Ellis and our relationship, often finding myself distracted by the idea that there might be something, or someone, better. A year after our daughter was born, I attended the Army Basic Non-Commissioned Officer (NCO) Course. While there, I met someone else, fell into what I thought was love, and decided I no longer wanted to be married. When I returned, I separated from Ellis and started the divorce process.

Our marriage was short-lived: three years and one month to the day. On July 1, 1991, we divorced. I was insatiable. Ellis wasn't a violent man, but I pushed him to the edge. I knew his triggers, and I used them like weapons.

I hurled words meant to wound, lashed out in anger, and sometimes struck first, daring him to hit me back because in my broken way of thinking, that kind of passion proved someone cared.

Ironically, the day we went to court was one of the happiest days of our marriage. We went together, side by side, laughing and making jokes about the other people in the courtroom. Despite everything, we were still friends. He loved me, and though I didn't fully realize it then, I loved him too.

Even after our divorce, we remained entangled in each other's lives. For ten years, whenever we spoke about each other, he was still my husband, and I was still his wife. Despite being divorced, we took care of one another. We confided in each other and supported each other. Whenever we were physically together, we moved as a family, as a couple, as husband and wife.

So why didn't we remarry? Fear. I was afraid that I was missing out on something better. He was afraid that I would hurt him again. We danced around each other, too scared to take the risk, too stubborn to admit what we both already knew. In January 2000, I had a realization: Ellis was my something better. He was the love I had been searching for all along. I did not want to give up what we were unwittingly building.

In an attempt to force his hand, I called him and said, *"This has got to end. Either we remarry, or we go our separate ways."*

He told me to do what I wanted.

Believing he was finished with me, that there was nothing left between us to salvage I made the difficult choice to move on.

Yet the truth is Ellis was never really gone. Our daughters kept us bound together, forcing us into constant communication, and over the years those conversations grew into something deeper than simple parental obligation. Even after our girls became adults and lived their lives separate from us, Ellis and I continued to call one another, to check in, to share the little details of life that only we seemed to understand.

What surprises many is that even through all the brokenness, we never stopped caring for each other. That love didn't vanish; it simply changed shape, softening into something enduring, something rooted in respect, history, and unshakable connection. Together with his wife, his partner of more than fifteen years, we are still family and friends. They have both stood beside me in ways few could ever imagine, especially in one of the darkest chapters of my life, the death of our youngest daughter.

No pain compares to your child preceding you in death, and in that unbearable season, when grief threatened to consume me, Celeste refused to let me walk through it alone. She stood by me. She protected me. His wife, with a grace and compassion that still humbles me, opened her heart not only to our grandchildren but to me as well. Together, they helped shoulder the weight of raising our oldest grandchild, our daughter's oldest child (she had five) pouring into her the love and stability she needed when her world was shaken.

To this day, I hold the deepest respect and gratitude for his wife. She could have chosen resentment or distance, but instead, she chose understanding, kindness, and a generosity of spirit that spoke louder than words. Her love for Ellis and her willingness to extend that love outward to our family, to me, became a testament to the kind of woman she is. Because of her, what might have been fractured beyond repair instead became a bond built on trust, mutual respect, and shared purpose.

## CHAPTER 6

# JUST BE GOOD

*"...Although I want to do good, evil is right there with me." ~**Romans 7:21b***

I can't tell you how I first knew there was a heaven and a hell, a God and a devil. No one taught me, at least not in words but somehow, it was planted in me before I could spell my own name. Maybe it came from my grandmother, though she never spoke of salvation. On Sunday mornings, after weekends thick with the scent of liquor and the sound of slammed doors and sharp voices, she would turn on the radio to a church service.

I never knew if she actually wanted to listen or if it was just what happened to play at that hour. It was background noise in a house that had no conversations about Jesus, just a preacher's voice spilling through static while she cleaned up liquor bottles, ashtrays overflowing with cigarette butts, and remnants of drunken brawls that tore through the house like storms on Friday and Saturday nights before.

The only spiritual lesson I remember getting at home was: "The devil's gonna get you." It was said half as a warning, half as a joke, but it stuck. I first heard the devil's name in a different way on *The Flip Wilson Show*, where Flip, dressed as a character named Geraldine, who would do something wrong and laugh, "The devil made me do it."

Everyone else laughed too. I didn't. I was afraid. Not of going to hell as much as I was afraid of *not making it into heaven.* I don't know why I thought about it so much, it was just always there.

One night, sitting in my grandfather's car, I remember staring at the stars, wondering about what heaven looked like, who was there, what it felt like to belong there.

"Daddy, how do you go to heaven?" I asked.

Without a pause, he answered, "Just be good."

I didn't know what that meant. In my world, "being good" had nothing to do with right or wrong; it meant not being in the way. I could lie and be punished for it, tell the truth and be punished for that too. I could watch my grandmother slip money from my grandfather's secret stash without consequence, but if I touched it, I'd feel the leather of his belt.

Still, every time I messed up, the refrain returned: the devil's gonna get you. And that's why the church bus felt like salvation before I even understood the word. Every Sunday, it rumbled through the neighborhood, gathering up poor black kids and carrying us to a white church in a nearby neighborhood. I loved that bus. It promised escape, even for a few hours.

The church was big, the auditorium like a gym. The preacher's voice was strong, the music louder still, voices rising in praise until you could feel it in your chest. After worship, we'd split into classes by age, hear stories about Jesus, and eat snacks we could never afford with food stamps. That's where I learned there was more to heaven than "being good" there was salvation, and Jesus on the cross, and the warning that sin still led to hell.

So, I "got saved" every time I went to church, just to be sure. If I wanted anything in life, it was to go to heaven, even though my mother swore I'd never make it.

The only time I went to church and didn't end up getting saved was when I went with my mother because that's not what we went for. With her, church wasn't about Jesus; it was about fashion. Easter Sunday was the big debut, sometimes Mother's Day too, but Easter was non-negotiable. That was the one time of year we got brand-new clothes, and you better believe we were going to show them off.

My mother used to say we were "sharp as a tack," and she meant it. We'd walk into that sanctuary like it was a runway. But once the fashion show was over, the real suffering began. With her, there was no children's church, no snacks, no coloring books. Just *sit up straight and act like you've got some sense.*

And I hated it.

Church was boring. It was hot. I was hungry. It lasted forever. The preacher droned on in the way most old Black Baptist preachers did back then constantly repeating "Ain't He alright?" and "Naaaaw, I say aaaw, ha!" over and over, wheezing and flailing like he's two steps away from collapsing, making about as much sense as a chicken doing calculus.

I had no clue what he was talking about, and I'm pretty sure my mother didn't either, because most of the time she was asleep. As far as I could tell, the only reason we went was out of obligation or so everyone could see us in our new clothes.

It was a waste! The only other time I ever wore those "special" outfits was for school pictures. By junior high school, that all stopped. I guess I wasn't "cute" enough for her to show off anymore. Either that, or I had started wanting clothes she wasn't about to buy just for me to wear once or twice. Whatever the reason, the tradition of fashion-show Sundays faded out, and so did church.

In high school, was when we lived across the street from Ms. Ann. Ms. Ann went to church every Sunday and sang in the choir. Her daughter was the same age as my sister, and the two of them were inseparable, which gave me a natural excuse to spend as much time at her house as possible.

I'd often sit on her porch for hours, the summer air thick and heavy around us, listening as she spoke about life. Her words were steady, honest, and grounding, the kind of guidance I never received at home. Through her, I found Saint Mark Baptist Church, my first real church family. I sang in the choir too, made friends (got a boyfriend), and, for the first time, felt like I belonged somewhere. For the record, I didn't understand a word that preacher was saying either.

My mother hated it. She couldn't stand the bond I had with my neighbor, and her jealousy simmered just beneath the surface. It wasn't really about my boyfriend at church; he was just the weapon she used to wound me. One day, her words landed with the weight of a slap: "The only reason you go to church is because of that boy. And it doesn't matter anyway, because you're going to hell like the rest of us."

That night, I lay in bed staring at the ceiling, her sharp voice echoing in my ears. A part of me wondered if she might be right, but deep down, I knew better. I had been going to church long before there was a boy. I kept going because I wanted to be there, because it was the only place that felt like I could breathe.

The hymns, the familiar faces, the soft rustle of hymnals, even the preacher's wheezing, dramatic calls they all gave me a sense of belonging I hadn't known existed. And so, I kept showing up, kept getting saved, over and over, pressing the reset button on my soul, hoping that each time, maybe this time, it would finally stick.

What frustrated me most was I didn't understand the Bible. I loved reading and had tried reading it many times as a kid, but the King James language was a locked door I couldn't open. Years later, while stationed in Korea, I found a different kind of Bible, the New International Version. It read like real words, like something I could finally understand. That's when the pieces started to fit together.

The sun was shining that day, bright and steady, and for the life of me, nothing else in my life felt as important or as urgent as that moment, even though I wasn't expecting it. I wasn't waiting for anyone, didn't know true salvation was about to find me. But when two of my sergeants approached me outside the barracks at Camp Coiner, I was ready in a way I didn't fully understand. There was nothing else happening in my life, nothing else that demanded my attention, and somehow, that made me open, receptive to the truth they shared. It was a Saturday morning in 1989 that I got saved for the last time with understanding this time. I received the gift of salvation, and for the first time, I knew I didn't have to get saved again. But my life didn't magically change. I still lived raggedy, carrying grace like something fragile I wasn't sure how to hold, unsure how it would fit into the broken parts of me. Even so, the Holy Spirit remained, steady and patient, keeping me from falling too far, even when I didn't fully understand why.

It would be four years before I set foot in a church again. In truth, I had been drifting for much longer. My last semi-attempt at commitment to God had been back in basic training, almost five years earlier. But that was mostly to escape the drill sergeants for a couple hours. By the time I finally returned, my children had become the voice calling me back, the reason I knew I needed to try again. Deep down, I realized it wasn't just church I needed. What I didn't know I was longing for was a real relationship with Christ.

But I didn't know how to do that yet.

While I was stationed at Fort Jackson South Carolina as a drill sergeant, I began attending services faithfully, but outside those church walls, I was still living for the world. My weekends were filled with parties and late nights, only to be followed by Sunday mornings in the choir stand. By Monday, I was back in uniform, barking orders, and cursing like I had swallowed the dictionary of profanity. Nothing was off limits. My life was split wide open: soldier by day, churchgoer by Sunday, but never fully surrendered to God.

I used to tell myself that at least I was trying. I read my Bible from time to time. I started listening to gospel music, John P. Kee especially. His songs carried so much Scripture, that I half-joked, he was the one teaching me the Bible: *"We walk by faith," "Greater is He that is in me."* And by the time I was stationed in Germany the second time, I had fallen in love with the voices of, among others, Yolanda Adams, Dottie Peoples, and Kirk Franklin. Their songs were like light in a dark room, stirring something in me that I didn't yet have the courage to fully embrace. But John P. Kee was always my favorite. He was my go to. His past life mirrored my present.

While still at Fort Jackson, I was assigned temporary duty in Honduras for six months. Oddly enough, most of my time there was spent singing in the choir and attending church services. I loved the way worship filled the hot, humid air of that little chapel, the kind of heat that made your clothes cling to your skin, yet somehow made the sound of praise feel richer, heavier, almost tangible. My voice blended with others, rising like incense, and for a moment, I felt clean.

But when the music stopped, the battle inside of me only grew louder.

Still, Honduras gave me something I always longed for: family. We would gather outside the PX or the Cantina, crowding around the picnic tables. One person would start humming a line of a gospel song, and before long another would slip in with an alto, then someone else with the soprano. We weren't rehearsing; we were harmonizing straight from the soul. Those impromptu sessions turned strangers into kin. We laughed, we sang, and for a little while, we forgot how far we were from home.

I loved being with them, and I believe they loved me too or at least, they put up with me. Because there were moments when my anger and inner turmoil spilled out onto the very people I cherished most. I argued with my choir members, my church family, that little circle of believers who became my lifeline in a foreign land. None of us had our families or old friends with us in Honduras; we only had each other. And in spite of my flaws, they accepted me, they stayed, and together we became a family.

But even surrounded by that love, I was still torn. Drinking, promiscuity, filthy talk that was my reality. I wanted to live holy, but the grip of my old life was strong. I kept trying to do both, live for God and live for myself. It was like I was negotiating with Him, offering half of me while keeping the other half tucked away. And I kept up that tug-of-war for years.

By the time I left Fort Jackson and transitioned into that second tour in Germany, life had shifted again. This time, I wasn't going alone. I went back to Europe married to someone from the past.

Kenneth became husband number three. Carrying all my unresolved battles, my half-surrendered heart, and my need for love that always seemed to outpace my wisdom, I stepped into yet another chapter of my story.

# CHAPTER 7

# LAUNDROMAT

*"See that you do not despise one of these little ones. For I tell you that their angels in heaven always see the face of my Father in heaven." ~**Matthew 18:10***

The hum of the laundromat machines filled the air, mixing with the occasional chime of the doorbell as customers came and went. My mother stood in front of me, placing a handful of quarters into my small hands.

"Stay here with these clothes. I'll be right back," she said.

Then she was gone.

I was eleven years old, left alone with my baby sister, who was barely eighteen months old, scooting around the laundromat in her walker. I didn't question my mother's absence at first; I was used to her leaving. Instead, I focused on the task she had assigned me. Load the washer. Move the clothes to the dryer. I busied myself with the tasks, feeling a strange mix of pride and fear. Pride because I was capable, fear because I was alone.

Hours passed. The daylight faded, stretching long shadows across the tiled floor. I didn't have a watch, but I knew it had been too long. Other customers left, replaced by new ones. Still, my mother did not return. My stomach growled, and my sister whined, hungry and tired. Her diaper full.

When the dryers buzzed, I pulled out the warm clothes, placing them into one of the baskets with a rack on top. I liked those baskets. They had handles that made it easier to push. I stacked everything neatly and looked around.

She was still gone.

I had no money for the payphone, no one to call. But I knew we lived just a few streets away. With no other choice, I placed my sister in her walker and pushed her toward home. The wheels struggled against the cracks in the sidewalk, and my small arms ached from pushing her weight in a vehicle not meant for the task.

When I reached our house, I tried the door. Locked.

I swallowed the lump in my throat and turned toward my grandparents' home, praying to no one that someone was there. When I knocked, my grandfather opened the door, his eyes widening at the sight of me and my sister.

He let us in without a word. He didn't ask why we were alone, didn't question why my mother had abandoned us. He just let us in.

Later, when my mother finally returned to the laundromat and realized we were gone, she was furious. She stormed into my grandparents' house, her anger shaking the walls. Without hesitation, she handed me over to Skeet. He whipped me for leaving the laundromat, for taking matters into my own hands, for daring to seek safety. My grandfather stood silent, as he always did. I wondered if he wanted to intervene, or if he had simply learned, like I had, that no amount of protest mattered.

It wasn't the only time I'd be punished for mishandling the weight of adult responsibilities I wasn't yet equipped to carry. There were many.

There was one of the many times my grandmother was passed out drunk on the sofa, leaving me alone in a dark house. I must have been five or six. Terrified, I called one of her sisters, hoping for comfort, for safety. Her daughter, my second cousin, caught a taxi and came to stay with me that night, and I felt a flicker of relief. But the next day, I was chastised and ridiculed. I had broken the unspoken rule: never seek help, never expect support.

There was the time I woke up to find myself alone with my then two-year-old sister. The phone rang, my mother's voice sharp and impatient on the other end. "Get dressed. I'm sending someone to pick you up." I dressed my sister in a corduroy jumpsuit, not knowing, not understanding that corduroy was for winter, not summer. I was foolish, she told me. A stupid child who didn't even know how to dress a toddler.

Then there was the time I put too much soap in the washing machine. My mother's response was swift, a punch to the chest that stole my breath. Maybe if I had stayed at the laundromat that day, I would have known how to do laundry properly. Or maybe it wouldn't have mattered.

Maybe nothing I did was ever going to be enough. I wish I had known.

I learned early on that survival meant do what you are told, no questions asked. I was supposed to get somewhere, sit down, and be quiet. Keep my mouth closed. I was not supposed to protest. Not supposed to request help. Not supposed to seek love. I was a child, and children were to be seen, not heard.

But even in silence, I carried my own truth. And even in fear, I knew I deserved more than this.

So, I took it.

## CHAPTER 8

# I KNOW YOU ARE HER HUSBAND

*"Let each man have his own wife, and let each woman have her own husband." ~1 Corinthians 7:2b*

It was Christmastime, 1995. I was a Sergeant First Class, a former drill sergeant and a single mother of two daughters. which meant I could run a platoon and a household, but apparently not a love life. My marriage to Ellis had ended four years earlier, and I had orders for a Permanent Change of Station (PCS) back to Germany. But nothing had changed. I had managed to land myself in yet another dead-end relationship with a man who, as far as I could tell, had no plans to marry me or even commit to a decent Christmas gift.

As usual, I was feeling unfulfilled, and whenever that happened, I had a bad habit of taking a stroll down memory lane, checking in on old flames to see if there was still "room in the inn." Spoiler alert: there usually wasn't.

This time, I reached out to Kenneth. I didn't have his number, which should've been my cue to let sleeping dogs and old boyfriends lie. But no, I decided to get creative. I called his mother. Nothing says "terrible idea in progress" quite like tracking down an ex through his mama.

For some reason, she had always liked me. Maybe it was my manners, or maybe she just knew her son could use a woman with a little sense, emphasis on *little*, given what I was about to do. As we caught up, she mentioned that Kenneth had divorced his first wife, yes, *the same fiancée* who he'd used to humiliate me in that car years ago, and was now married to someone else.

That should've been the end of the story. Case closed. Do not pass "Go." But no, I needed those $200, so I let her take my number anyway, like I didn't already know where this train was headed.

A short while later, Kenneth called, and just like that, there I was again caught up in nostalgia with a large side of bad judgment. At the time, I was stationed in South Carolina and planning to drive home to Memphis for Christmas. My route went straight through Nashville. Of course, it did. All the trappings of stupid in motion. So naturally, we arranged to meet. I picked him up on my way, and together, we drove to Memphis, him grinning like this was destiny, and me quietly convincing myself that this wasn't the biggest mistake of the holiday season.

At some point during our visit, my mother, always one to offer incorrect, unsolicited advice, casually remarked, *"Y'all have been going back and forth since high school. I don't know why you don't just go ahead and get married."*

That was all it took.

On the way back, instead of dropping Kenneth off in Nashville, we stopped just long enough for him to grab some personal belongings, and then he came with me to South Carolina. The plan was simple: he would send divorce papers to his wife, she would sign them, and then we would get married. After all, the only way he could come with me to Germany was as my husband. He assured me that his marriage was already falling apart and that it was just a matter of making it official.

But when he presented her with the divorce papers, she refused to sign them. She wouldn't even consider it unless he came back to Nashville to talk to her in person. But Kenneth refused to go back. He had made up his mind that he was staying with me.

And so, instead of waiting, we took a different route. South Carolina didn't have a system to check marriage records across state lines, so we got married there while he was still legally married to her. That was the beginning of the end.

We were married on February 10, 1996. From the very beginning, our relationship was volatile like living inside a storm that never stopped circling back on itself. For five long, exhausting months, we fought constantly. Every conversation turned into an argument. Every silence was loaded with resentment. One night, in a fit of rage, he bought a bus ticket and went back to Nashville.

During that time, I discovered I was pregnant. But our relationship was so fractured, so toxic, I made the painful decision to get another abortion. I couldn't bear the thought of being connected to him for the rest of my life. Still, he kept calling, and I foolishly, weakly kept answering. In a moment I still regret, I drove to Nashville and picked him up again. I should have left him there.

I don't know what I expected from marrying another woman's husband, but the consequences of that betrayal came swift and merciless. From the moment we said "I do," he took over my life. He forbade me from speaking to my friends in the community I had built in South Carolina. He threw away clothes with my former last name from my marriage to Ellis, as though erasing my past could secure his place in my present.

Kenneth had always had issues with authority. He'd been discharged from the Army for misconduct, his rebellion catching up with him, his pride too big to fit inside anyone's rules. As a Senior NCO, a former drill sergeant, someone who thrived within the structure and discipline of the military, I represented everything he despised. He never missed a chance to remind me of it.

*"You're not in charge of me,"* he snapped. *"I'm not one of your soldiers. You can't tell me what to do."*

His resentment turned quickly into hostility, and his hostility into violence.

We fought from Columbia, South Carolina, all the way to Grafenwöhr, Germany. We fought in the hotel on the way there, in the guest house while waiting for our quarters, and in our new home once we finally settled. It didn't matter what

I said, everything I said was "me trying to tell him what to do." And if I'm honest, maybe I was. That's who I was, a leader. I gave orders. I took charge.

As crazy as it sounds, I think I would have kept fighting him just to stay in the marriage. Some small, broken part of me believed that because we'd been high school sweethearts, we were meant to be together. Because of the way our relationship began, I convinced myself I *deserved* the abuse. In my mind, that was what love looked like: messy, painful, consuming.

But then he did the unthinkable. He attempted to destroy my career, my livelihood.

In a twisted attempt to gaslight me and to make himself look noble, he went behind my back to my chain of command. After one of our fights, he visited my Company Commander, telling her we were "having marital problems" and that he was willing to "go to counseling or even leave" if it would help me focus on my job.

I found out because an NCO from the orderly room, a man who barely knew me, called to ask why my husband was in the office meeting with leadership. He said, "Sergeant Mayes, why is your husband coming to see the company commander?" I told him to call me when Kenneth left.

When I got that call, I walked straight to my First Sergeant's office and told him everything. I told him I was afraid for my life, for my daughter's life, and for my career. I explained that my husband was trying to make me look unstable to make it appear that *I* was the problem. To destroy the twelve-year military career, I had fought tooth and nail to build.

God was there with me that day. I know He was. I felt His presence when I told the First Sergeant. He didn't question me. He didn't hesitate. Right there in his office, he called housing and arranged for a key to a safe house.

The Military Police escorted me to my home so I could pack up our things, my clothes, my daughter's clothes and then they took us to that safe house. We stayed hidden there all weekend while they expedited an Early Return of Dependents order to send Kenneth back to the United States. The same NCO who had warned me escorted him to the airport.

Even in leaving, he couldn't resist taking something from me. Before he left, he sold my car, stole the brand-new clothes I'd just bought for my children and my phone card, as if he needed to rob me one last time.

Months later, his wife, the woman he'd left behind when he came to Germany called me. Apparently, he'd confessed after she'd demanded to know where he had been for the past nine months, and when he told her, she called me for the truth. She didn't believe we had actually gotten married. I told her everything. I apologized. I didn't know what it would fix, but I told her anyway.

A short while later, using that stolen calling card, he called me one last time. *"If you divorce me, I'll make your life hell,"* he warned. But I had already been to hell with him and I wasn't planning to stay there. I went to a German attorney and filed for divorce through the local court.

This time, when he left my life, it was for good. I never saw him again. And though the pain was still raw and the fear still lingered, I could feel God's presence wrapping around me quietly, steady, mercifully drawing me closer and closer to Him. He had carried me out of that darkness, even when I didn't think I deserved to be saved. It was then that my relationship with and my understanding of Him began to truly evolve.

## CHAPTER 9

# JUST GET A DIVORCE

*Make allowance for each other's faults, and forgive anyone who offends you. Remember, the Lord forgave you, so you must forgive others.* **~Colossians 3:13**

I had been in Germany for about nine months, and once again, I found myself entangled in another adulterous relationship. My work was in the strength management office, where I served as the NCO responsible for managing the slots versus personnel for my unit. There was a civilian lady who worked as the administrative assistant to the Major who was over our section.

This civilian lady, Miss Rhyse, was a devoted Christian who attended chapel services regularly. Occasionally, I would join the Sunday service, though my attendance was inconsistent, and my life was far from aligned with her faith. I loved to sing; it was my natural expression of joy. Whenever I was happy, it showed in my voice.

One day, as I was singing in the office, Miss Rhyse, who always complimented my singing, encouraged me to come to church with the phrase, "It's a shame you don't use that voice for the Lord." Most of the time, I went because of her persistent encouragement. She had an uncanny way of noticing everything happening around her, and she always paid attention to me.

Miss Rhyse was married to a soldier in a different unit, and she had a young son. She watched me quietly, making small, seemingly casual comments, what I now recognize were seeds of faith, gently planted. "You should come to church," she would say, or she would invite me to some chapel event. She didn't do this with anyone else, it seemed just me. One day, out of the blue, she approached me at her desk and asked, with a mixture of concern and gentle firmness, why I didn't attend church more consistently. She could see the life I was living and didn't shy away from confronting it.

"You're wasting your heart," she said. "He's not going to leave his wife, and you're only hurting yourself." Her words struck me straight to the core. We were in the office; she had no idea what was truly going on in my mind, yet it was as if she could see my soul. I turned to her and admitted quietly, "I know."

"You should surrender your life to Christ," she said.

"I know," I replied, "but I'm not ready to give up the world."

It would take years for me to see the truth: I had become addicted to acceptance and validation. In the twisted logic of my heart, I convinced myself that if he could betray his wife, it meant I mattered, that I was someone, that I was enough. I clung desperately to that illusion, mistaking his fleeting attention for love, his choices for proof of my worth. In doing so, I lost myself in the shadows of a longing that could never be satisfied.

Still, she persisted. She offered me kindness, encouragement, and a watchful, patient presence. Every time I saw her, it was like a small punch of grace, a kind, persistent reminder that there was more for me beyond the chaos I was living in. I resisted, sometimes sarcastically, but she never stopped, and I am forever grateful to God that she didn't.

One day, in December, she invited me to a New Year's Eve service. I had been in Germany for a year and a half. It was my second Christmas there and I was feeling low. My boyfriend hadn't come to see me on Christmas as I expected, and I was heartbroken. I packed up my two daughters, ages seven and ten, and we went to Miss Rhyse's home. We spent the next two days there, attending the service and sitting in her living room afterward, talking about life, faith, and change.

During the service, I felt things around me that I did not understand, an unexplainable presence, spiritual activity that I later realized was linked to gifts I had: discernment and prophecy. That night and the next day, we read the Bible, prayed, and discussed the transformations I needed in my life. Miss Rhyse helped me understand Christianity in a profoundly simple way: being a Christian wasn't about rituals; it was about having a relationship with Jesus, walking with Him daily, like a partnership.

I told her I wanted to give up my sinful ways, particularly my relationship with the married man and smoking. She laughed lightly and with a healthy dose of disgust she said, "You'll have to ask Mr. Rhyse (that's how she referred to him when speaking about him to others) how to do that. I never did that nasty mess."

When Mr. Rhyse overheard, he asked, "Sergeant Mayes, do you want to quit smoking?" I admitted I did, and he simply said, "Well, just keep on smoking." What?! "You'll have to give it to God. Only He can take it from you." He continued.

The next morning, I went home determined. I didn't call my usual friends. I wanted to separate myself from everything that had kept me bound. In my apartment, I set the stage for what I hoped would be one last smoke. I made a good meal, grabbed my ice-cold Coca-Cola, and sat by the cracked bathroom window, the way I always did. I lit the cigarette and prayed the entire time I smoked.

"Lord, please take this nasty habit away from me. I don't want to smoke anymore, but it tastes so good. Please deliver me? Because only You can." By the time I reached the end of that cigarette, tears were falling. I whispered, "In Jesus' name, amen." It was January 2, 1997. That was the last cigarette I ever smoked.

I also ended the adulterous relationship. I asked the man to come over, under the pretense of spending time together. When he arrived, I stood on the sidewalk in front of my house and looked him straight in the face. "I can't do this anymore," I said. "I want to live for Christ."

He made a curt remark and walked away. That was the end of that chapter.

I sold all my secular CDs, Jodeci, Boyz II Men, Keyshia Cole, and replaced them with John P. Kee, Yolanda Adams, Kirk Franklin and the likes. I immersed myself in the Bible, commentaries, and study guides. Slowly, my life began to change: the clubbing, drinking, and promiscuity stopped, and I started walking more closely with God.

During this period, I reconnected with Deborah, a fellow soldier I had met earlier while trying to recover the car Kenneth sold on his way out. Deborah had a husband, two young children, and a heart steeped in faith. We became fast friends. She had been raised in the church and knew how to pray, understand Scripture, and live a life aligned with God's word. She was funny and down to earth. I stayed close to her because I wanted to learn, and she became a spiritual sister to me.

Through our church community, we built a family of our own. It included her husband, our children, my sister and others like Joanna, an Army wife with five children, a young mother across the hall with a frequently deployed infantry husband, and the Air Force, childless couple who headed the youth ministry. Together, we supported each other, grew in faith, and created a nurturing, loving environment.

Deborah's influence on me was profound. One day, during a slumber party she had hosted for my daughter,

I complained, probably for the hundredth time, about something my mother had done. This time expressing my hatred towards her. Deborah looked me straight in the eye and asked, *"So let me get this straight. You're going to go to hell because of what someone else did to you?"*

That moment pierced me, and I knew I had to start forgiving, not just my mother, but everyone I felt had wronged me.

But old habits have a way of creeping back in. I fell again into promiscuous behavior when a single man from the church developed a crush on me. Eventually, word got out about my relationship with him, and the chaplain asked me to step down from teaching children's church. I mistakenly blamed Deborah for this, though she had been a true friend and mentor to me, challenging me to forgive, grow, and reconcile with my mother and others I had held resentment against.

Why I thought she would betray me this way is beyond me. She had always supported me and been my closest ally and I rejected her. Just like my mother had taught me. *"If it doesn't work out you can just get a divorce."* Cutting people out of my life had become my MO.

By the time Deborah prepared to leave Germany, I had grown tremendously in faith and knowledge of God. However, signing her paperwork as the now Outprocessing NCO, broke my heart; she was my dearest friend, yet I completed the task silently, like she meant nothing. Shortly after, I faced further challenges with the military, was reduced from E7 to E6 under UCMJ authority, and prepared for a PCS move to Washington State.

But through every trial, the steadfast friendships of Miss Rhyse, Deborah, and my wider church family, along with my half-hearted surrender to Christ, began to reshape me. Slowly, my faith, my choices, and my very life were being transformed.

## CHAPTER 10

# A DESPERATE YES

*"Trust in the* L<small>ORD</small> *with all your heart and lean not on your own understanding." ~****Proverbs 3:5***

The second time I saw Russell, he was leaning out of the window of his sister, Elaine's, house. The place was still under construction, the skeletal wooden frame of a second floor stretching toward the sky, jagged and unfinished.

I had just arrived in Washington, and my daughters and I immediately reconnected with Elaine. Elaine and I went way back. We were stationed together in Garlstedt, Germany, during my very first overseas tour, back when I was married to Terrance. That's when I first met her. Years later, when I learned I'd be stationed at Fort Lewis, Washington, I immediately thought of her. I knew she was there, so I called to reconnect and let her know I'd soon be arriving.

Back when I was in Garlstedt, pregnant with my first child, Elaine had been my anchor. She'd recently had a beautiful baby girl who was about two years old by the time I was expecting, and she took me under her wing. Her mother lived with her in Germany, helping care for her daughter, and together they gave me a kind of refuge, a soft place to land when life was rough.

I was living with her when I gave birth, and she was right there with me in the delivery room. Not long after, when I needed an emergency appendectomy, Elaine was there again, helping me, caring for my baby, even bringing her to the hospital to see me. I've never forgotten that. She was pure kindness wrapped in calm strength, and I've always appreciated her deeply for it.

Russell looked down at me with a strange certainty in his eyes, and without any preamble, he asked, "Will you marry me?"

I said *yes*.

Not because I loved him. Not because I really even knew him. But because weeks earlier, in a moment of quiet desperation, I had whispered a prayer to God: *"Lord, the next man who asks me to marry him... I will."*

It wasn't faith exactly. It wasn't even surrender. It was more like a hope wrapped tightly in despair, a deep craving to be chosen, covered, protected. Because of my relationship with Elaine, it somehow felt... inevitable.

Russell had nothing: no job, no home, no plan. Seventeen years in prison for drug-related charges including addiction, had left him adrift, a man trying to grow roots in a world that had long since moved on without him. He was living in a camper in his sister's driveway, trying to piece together a life. And I, a woman who had already been married three times and desperate, said *yes*. Ugh! It is sickening now to think of how desperate it was.

My daughters and I arrived in Fort Lewis, Washington, on Sunday, July 11, 1999. We checked into the post guest house, and that Monday morning I began my search for a place to live.

At the very first apartment complex I visited, I met a young couple from Sarasota, Florida. They were there to see the same units I was. As luck would have it, there were two apartments available. One on the first floor and one in the basement. The leasing agent showed us both. I took the first floor; they took the basement.

Because of the broken relationships in Germany and the UCMJ action I had just received; I had made a firm declaration to myself that I would not be making any new friends or forming any new relationships outside of Elaine. I had decided that connection was trouble, and I was determined to keep my circle the size of a period.

The young wife's name was Lydia. She was 18, barely out of high school, and newly married to an Army soldier. This was her first time living away from home, and she had no family or friends nearby. Her husband had his unit, his work, his mission. She had no one. So naturally, she started coming upstairs to spend time with my daughters and me.

No matter how hard I tried to keep my distance, Lydia just kept showing up with that bubbly, persistent friendliness that made it impossible to stay guarded. One day, she even gave me her phone number and asked about my plans for

Thanksgiving, which, in my mind, was utterly ridiculous since Thanksgiving was *four months away*. But she was young, she was lonely, and she meant well. I, on the other hand, was emotionally bankrupt, my emotional IQ at the time was somewhere around negative zero. I was focused on survival, not friendship.

That all changed one night. I was working a second job doing inventory, because I was still financially recovering from the rank reduction and forfeiture of pay the Army had sent me home from Germany with as a "parting gift."

We'd all meet up in the parking lot of a bookstore, pile into a van, and head to our assigned location to count boxes until dawn. Then, bleary-eyed and half-delirious from counting things that probably didn't even need to be counted, we'd ride back and go our separate ways.

But one night, when we returned, my van was gone. Not just *any* van, my *brand-new* van. The one with only 21 miles on it. Gone. Vanished. The parking spot was empty.

The moment I realized my daughters were home alone, panic hit me like a freight train. My mind started spinning, what if something had happened, what if someone broke in, what if, then suddenly, I remembered: Lydia. She had given me her phone number earlier that very day. Thank God she had, and thank God, I had actually remembered it.

I called her, voice trembling, and without hesitation she ran upstairs to my apartment to sit with my girls until I got home. She stayed with them until I walked through the door, calm as could be, like she'd been sent there by an angelic dispatch service.

It was Lydia who drove me to pick up my van when it was finally found. It was Lydia who took me to the dealership when I needed help sorting it out. It was Lydia who gave me rides, watched my kids, and showed up for me again and again. The same Lydia I'd tried *so hard* not to be friends with.

After that night, there was no separating us. We became joined at the hip, and the heart. We started going to the same church, singing in the choir together, learning all the songs side by side. She prayed with me and prayed *for* me, especially that I'd find someone of my own. So, when Russell asked me to marry him, Lydia was thrilled.

Because of her loving, kind, forgiving spirit, she never saw his flaws. She only saw a man who seemed to love me, who seemed to care for me. When I look back now, I believe he did. He just didn't know how, and neither did I.

Like me, Russell carried the weight of an emotionally charged childhood. You could see it in his eyes, in the way he talked about his mother with both tenderness and pain. His life had been marked by disappointment, by the ache of wanting more but never knowing how to ask for it.

He was always trying to do something for me, even when I didn't want help, even when I didn't know how to receive it. He gave the best of what he had, which, in hindsight, was a lot more than I recognized at the time.

Once, I bought a little chair for five dollars at a yard sale, intending to refurbish it myself. Before I could even get my tools out, he'd quietly done it for me. Another time, I was trying to cover the carpet in my van with plastic to protect it from stains, he swooped right in and took over that project too.

What he meant as an act of love, I took as interference. I saw control where there was only care. I don't think I ever really gave him a fair chance.

But Lydia, just eighteen years old, saw him clearly. She saw him with her heart. She'd say, *"He really loves you. He just wants to help. Let him."* But I was too bitter, too broken, too *everything* to see what she saw.

And still, Lydia stood by me when I said *I do*. To the man with no job, no home, and no plan.

Even Elaine, his sister, gently said, *"You know you don't have to do this, right?"*

But I felt like I did because of that prayer. That desperate, ill-conceived promise I'd made to God. We married exactly one month later, on Valentine's Day, in a small church in Lakewood, Washington.

The day before, I had prayed for the rapture. I begged God to take me before I had to go through with it. But no lightning split the sky, no angel descended, no trumpet sounded.

So, the next day, I took a deep breath, squared my shoulders, and reluctantly walked down the aisle.

Just two weeks before our wedding, I was discharged from the military.

Suddenly, the structure that had ordered my days, the thing that told me who I was, where to be, and what to do was gone. I had no plan, no roadmap, only a faint, trembling hope that maybe, somehow, I could find stability again in my life, and in this marriage, I was walking into with more fear than faith.

But almost immediately, everything began to unravel.

Russell moved into the apartment with me and my girls, and it didn't take long for tension to fill every inch of that small space. It felt like he resented my friendship with Lydia, the very person that rallied for him, like the warmth and laughter we shared somehow threatened him. Slowly, he began to take over my life just as Kenneth once had.

We argued constantly. Sometimes I couldn't even tell you what started it, something small, something meaningless but it would ignite into an endless, exhausting battle. Russell didn't argue to resolve; he argued to *win*. His voice would carry through the walls, through the night, until exhaustion took the place of peace.

Sometimes, just to get a few hours of rest, I'd go to sleep in my daughters' room. It was the only safe space left to breathe. But even then, he would knock on the walls, tapping or pounding just enough to remind me that escape was impossible. That I was going to listen, that I was going to answer him.

Because as loving and sweet as Russell could sometimes be, he could also turn into the complete opposite angry, unpredictable, even violent. It was like living with two men in one body: one who wanted to love me, and another who wanted to break me down.

The apartment was small, too small for that kind of storm. There was nowhere to hide, nowhere to regroup. And yet, I kept telling myself that things would somehow work themselves out. This was my fourth marriage. It *had* to work. It just had to. I couldn't bear the shame or exhaustion of another failure.

That same year, my mother was turning fifty and threw herself a grand party in Memphis. My sister, always the peacemaker, bought me a plane ticket, practically forcing a reconciliation I wasn't ready for. I hadn't wanted to go. I felt too raw, too worn, too buried under the weight of everything unraveling around me.

But my sister's plan worked. I went. I showed up. And something unexpected happened. In Memphis, I met people. I networked. I felt the faint stirrings of possibility again like maybe life hadn't completely given up on me after all. Within weeks, opportunity opened up, and I made the decision to move there with my girls.

Russell stayed behind for surgery; his absence was a quiet telling of what was to come.

\*\*\*

When I first arrived in Memphis, the girls and I moved in with my mother. We stayed there for about three months, long enough for me to catch my breath and try to rebuild some kind of life from the pieces I had left. My first order of business was to find a church home, and of course, it had to be Church of God in Christ (COGIC). That's where I had spent the last four years learning, growing, and that's where I felt most comfortable.

COGIC was familiar, it was where I had learned to pray through my pain, where the music could lift me right out of whatever darkness I was in, and where I could lose myself in worship without judgment. It was the kind of church where the Word was preached with fire, where the Spirit moved freely, and where you could run, dance, or shout without fear of being ushered out for your praise.

It was a place that felt alive. Even though I never claimed the title of being "COGIC," I knew that's where I could find what I needed most, healing, connection, and strength to start over. It was a place where I had found family. After visiting a few churches, I finally found one that felt like home and settled in.

Russell followed about a month later. By the time he arrived, the first threads of control were already wrapping themselves around me, soft at first, almost invisible, but tightening with time. At first, I told myself that maybe this new beginning in a new city would help us find peace. But even before we moved out of my mother's house, the warning signs were already flashing.

There were arguments, sharp words that cut deep, shouting that shook the walls, and nights when the police had to be called. One cycle of chaos after another. I kept telling myself it was just the stress of transition, that once we had our own place things would calm down, that we'd finally be okay. But deep down, I knew better. Peace didn't follow him, or me, it disappeared wherever we went.

When I got a new job, one that offered life insurance, I thought I was doing something good, something responsible when I tried to provide coverage for our family, for him as my spouse. He exploded! He accused me of planning to kill him. I remember standing there, stunned, trying to make sense of the accusation, before realizing that I had stumbled into the deep waters of his paranoia, something I hadn't fully seen before.

In hindsight, I think he carried pieces of prison with him everywhere he went. The walls, the suspicion, the hypervigilance it all came with him, invisible but heavy. Probably some form of PTSD, though I didn't have that language for it then.

It wasn't just the life insurance. He would get angry if I tried to joke with him or play any kind of harmless prank. What I thought was teasing, he took as betrayal. What I thought was laughter, he took as a threat. It was like living with a man whose mind was always braced for attack.

When we finally found our own apartment, Russell found work at a casket-making company. For a little while, it seemed like we might actually find our footing. But the paranoia and control followed us right through the front door.

At first, it was small questions that seemed harmless. *Where are you going? Who are you talking to? When will you be back?* But soon, those questions built invisible walls around me. His curiosity hardened into control, his affection into surveillance.

After joining the church, I immediately became part of the choir, directed by Patrick and his brother, who served as the minister of music. Patrick got on my nerves constantly. He was always fussing at the alto section, demanding that we sing louder or complaining that we were off key. I gave it everything I had, nearly losing my voice sometimes, but somehow it was never enough. I didn't hesitate to let him know when I didn't appreciate being yelled at. I wasn't afraid to speak my mind if I didn't like a song I'd been assigned to lead, or if a song I recommended was handed to someone else.

I never saw Patrick as anything more than my choir director. I wasn't attracted to him in the slightest. But when his brother casually asked Russell if I was difficult to get along with, Russell lost it. His jealousy ignited, wild and irrational. He accused me of having an affair with *them* and began monitoring my every move at church. Before long, he forbade me from participating in any choir activities outside of Sunday service. He wouldn't let me go on church trips, and I couldn't even attend service without him. His jealousy burned hot and fast, flaring anytime another man so much as looked my way. Even God's house wasn't safe from his suspicion.

His love, if it was love, was suffocating. It tangled itself around me, heavy with anger, insecurity, and fear. He was possessive, unpredictable. Then, there was the gambling. He was always gone. At first, I thought it was work or stress, but then I learned the truth: addiction doesn't disappear. It just shifts shape.

For Russell, it shifted into the flashing lights and hollow promises of casinos. He would create an argument so he would have a reason to storm out, vanish for hours, and come home with empty pockets and a silence so thick it filled the room before he did.

I didn't know how to love him, and truthfully, I don't think he knew how to love anyone. His childhood had carved deep scars into his soul. His mother's rejection, her resentment of the very light skin he was born in, a daily reminder of her own infidelity had left wounds he never healed. He grew up trying to earn love from someone who saw him as a living mistake. That kind of pain doesn't just disappear it seeps into everything.

We were two broken people trying to build something whole, each one hoping the other could fix what life had shattered.

Once, on a road trip to visit his family in Michigan, he tried to surprise me. He knew my favorite restaurant was a hundred miles off our route, and while I was sleeping, he quietly changed directions, thinking he was doing something sweet, something thoughtful.

But when I woke up and saw that we were completely off course, something inside me snapped. It wasn't just irritation, it was panic disguised as rage. I felt the walls closing in, the familiar sense that I was no longer in control of my own life. I grabbed the nearest thing, a hardback book and began hitting him in the head with it, over and over, my daughters sleeping in the backseat.

He swerved wildly, trying to steer with one hand, to block my blows with the other, to shout over my screaming, to keep the van from spinning out on the highway. My daughters woke up crying, yelling for us to stop, their voices blending with the roar of the tires and the chaos inside the van.

When he finally managed to pull over, the van jerked from side to side before coming to a stop on the shoulder. He jumped out, leaving the driver's door flung wide open, wind rushing in from the highway. In one frantic motion, he slid open the van's side door, lunging toward me. I was in the backseat, and he tried to drag me out to pull me into the street, to make me fight him out there on the side of the road.

I twisted and scrambled, sliding between the seats, trying to get to the front. All I could think about was getting behind the wheel, taking off, leaving him there on the asphalt. But he grabbed for the door, and I pulled it back. I was screaming for my daughters to help me close it, my hands shaking, my heart pounding so hard it drowned out the traffic. Cars whipped by us at seventy miles an hour, horns blaring. We could have been killed at any moment, and still, we fought.

It was chaos, pure, suffocating chaos. Somehow, by some miracle, we gathered ourselves enough to make it to a gas station. When he stopped to pump gas, I ran inside and begged the cashier to call the police. The words tumbled out before I could even think. I told them he had assaulted me and my girls. It wasn't the full truth, it wasn't the truth at all, but it was the only way I knew to get free in that moment.

The police came, questioned him, and held him long enough for me to grab the keys and drive away. My hands trembled the entire time. I drove the rest of the way to Michigan alone, my daughters silent in the back, the air heavy with everything that had just happened.

When we arrived, I went straight to his sister's house. I told her everything: the fighting, the chaos, the fear. She listened quietly, her eyes full of concern and something else I couldn't quite name. When I finished, she spoke softly but firmly, with a kind of love that still cut deep. She reminded me that I had chosen him, that I knew the challenges he carried, how he had only recently been released from prison and that it was now my duty as his wife to fix my marriage.

I remember sitting there numb, her words sinking like stones. Still, I listened. The next day, I packed up my daughters, got back in the car, and drove ten long hours home to my apartment, to my husband.

To this day, I still don't fully understand why I was so angry. Maybe it wasn't him I was fighting, it was myself.

Maybe I never really liked him. Maybe I was furious that I had married him at all. Every detour, every wrong turn, every moment off course felt like proof that I had lost control again. That my life wasn't my own.

Maybe the hardest truth of all was that I had married him because I believed God told me to.

But He hadn't. It was a lie, a desperate, misguided attempt to turn my longing into purpose. And that belief, misunderstood and misplaced, became the fragile thread holding everything together, even as the walls of our marriage crumbled around us.

Little did I know that the moment I struck him first, I had opened a door I could never close. In that instant, I had set something in motion, an unspoken permission for the pain to turn physical, for anger to take on a new and terrifying shape. After that night, his rage no longer stayed behind words or slammed doors. It took form. It found my body.

One night, during yet another argument that spiraled out of control, our words became weapons. Mine were sharp and trembling, his were low, deliberate, and dangerous. The air between us was electric, thick with all the things we couldn't say without breaking something. I remember the blur of his movement before I even realized what was happening, the sudden rush of air, the shock of the floor meeting my back, and then the crushing weight that followed.

His feet were on my chest, pressing, twisting, pinning me down as if to erase the part of me that still dared to resist him. Pain radiated through my ribs, spreading like fire beneath my skin. My breath came shallow and ragged, my eyes fixed on the ceiling, tracing the faint cracks as if they might offer a way out. My heart beat frantically against his soles, each thump a reminder that I was still alive, though I wasn't sure why.

When I finally managed to free myself, I stumbled downstairs, shaking uncontrollably, and locked myself in a small room in the back of the house. I slid to the floor and curled into a ball, pulling my knees to my chest as though I could make myself disappear. The silence that followed was deafening, broken only by my sobs and the sound of my own breathing, uneven and desperate.

That night, I cried myself to sleep on the sofa, the taste of salt and shame heavy on my tongue. I didn't know it then, but that moment would haunt me for years, not just because of what he did, but because of what I had unleashed when I first crossed that line. But, I sucked it up. I had made my bed; I was determined to lay in it.

When his teenage daughter moved in with us, everything shifted. The tension that had been simmering beneath the surface finally exploded. That was the beginning of the end.

He let her do whatever she wanted: no school, no rules, no consequences. My children didn't get that kind of freedom. They still had structure, expectations, discipline, and every time I tried to bring some balance into the house, it turned into a battle.

One night, I decided we needed to come together to talk like a family, to find some kind of peace. I called a family meeting, hoping we could clear the air. But Russell didn't like that I set boundaries for his daughter. He accused me of verbally attacking her, of being unfair, of treating her differently. His words stung, twisting the truth until I sounded like the villain. The conversation dissolved into shouting, and one by one, everyone scattered to their rooms, everyone except him.

I stayed in the kitchen, exhausted and trembling, trying to finish baking a cake for my youngest daughter's birthday party the next day. She had planned it for weeks, excited to celebrate with her friends. All I wanted was to give her that small joy. But he sat on the steps just a few feet away, taunting me with his words poking, prodding, knowing exactly how to break me down.

Something in me cracked. Out of sheer frustration and exhaustion, I grabbed a spatula and threw it at him. It didn't even hit him but that was all the reaction he needed. The moment he saw my anger flare, it was like I'd handed him permission. He came for me, fast, his hands around my throat, shaking me so hard the room blurred.

I fought back kicking, pushing, clawing for air until my daughter came running from her room, screaming. I stumbled toward her door, trying to get inside, but he grabbed me just as I was closing it. In that split second, my daughter, my brave, terrified little girl snatched one of her basketball trophies from the dresser and swung it with all her strength.

The trophy hit him square in the forehead. I can still hear the sound of it, the sharp crack, the quick gasp that followed. Blood poured down his face. He staggered backward, stunned, and finally retreated.

My hands were shaking as I called the police. Then I called my mother and my sister, who was visiting home on leave from the military. By the time they arrived, I was outside, still talking to the officers, trying to explain what had happened, still trembling from the adrenaline.

When the police finished questioning everyone, they made a decision that broke me completely. They arrested everyone who had taken part in the altercation, including my eleven-year-old daughter.

I will never forget my mother's face: her fury, her disbelief. "She could have killed him!" she yelled, her voice cracking as they placed me in handcuffs.

I had never been arrested before, not since juvenile detention when I was sixteen. I never imagined I would see the inside of a jail cell again. But that night, I did.

The holding cell was cold and crowded with seventeen women crammed into one room. There was one metal toilet in the corner, out in the open. No privacy, no dignity. I held it for hours, unwilling to expose myself like that. Some of the others didn't. We all turned away, pretending not to see, trying to maintain a shred of humanity in a place where there was none.

Some women ranted incoherently, their voices slurred with alcohol or drugs. Others cried quietly. A few slept curled on the floor like children. I sat on a narrow bench, knees pulled to my chest, staring at the concrete wall, my mind looping the same question over and over: *How did I get here?*

Fifteen years in the military. Two daughters. I had traveled the world. I had led soldiers. I had built a life from nothing, and now, I was sitting in jail, orange jumpsuit, plastic mattress, plastic pillow, accused of violence in my own home, for something I felt I didn't even start.

By morning, they finally booked me. The sound of the metal door slamming behind me still echoes in my memory. They placed me in a pod of twenty cells lined down a narrow hall, each holding two bunk beds. I was assigned to a cell at the very end, sharing it with a woman whose face I never saw. She slept with her back to me the entire time, her body motionless, her silence haunting.

Lying there on that hard plastic mattress, I stared at the ceiling and tried to make sense of it all. I replayed every decision, every compromise, every ignored red flag that led me here. The weight of it pressed down on me until I could barely breathe. I wanted to blame him, to blame the system, to blame anyone but myself. But deep down, I knew I had ignored too many warnings, justified too many wrongs in the name of love, or at least what I thought love was.

As I lay there, lost in thought, something stirred outside my cell. A guard's voice echoed through the pod, lecturing the women about responsibility. I only caught fragments at first, but then her words grew sharper, clearer, cutting through my shame.

She said that none of us could blame anyone else for where we were. Even if we were there because of someone else's actions, it was *our choice* to be around that person, to stay in that situation, to ignore what we already knew. And because of that choice, we had to own the consequences.

Her words hit me like a revelation. They sank deep into the hollow space inside me, the one I had been filling with anger and excuses. I realized she was right. I had chosen to stay. I had chosen to believe lies, to chase healing in a man instead of in God.

So, I prayed harder than I had ever prayed. I asked God to help me understand why I kept repeating the same patterns. Why I couldn't find a husband who loved me. As I prayed, He led me to a scripture that felt like a whisper straight to my soul:

*"For your Maker is your husband; the Lord of hosts is His name."* Isaiah 54:5

I wept quietly into my pillow, the verse echoing in my spirit until exhaustion overtook me.

When I woke, I heard the sound of keys turning in the lock. The guard's voice called my name.

I was being released on my own recognizance.

As the door opened, I stepped out shaken, hollow, and strangely free. Somewhere between the bars and the scripture, I felt God was sending me a message I did not want to hear: *"I, your Maker, am that husband."*

When I was released, I didn't go home. I went to my mother's. My daughter sat beside me that night, her young voice filled with wisdom beyond her years. *"Mommy, this reminds me of a book."* She told me about *The Frog King*, a story about a kingdom that begged for a king, only to regret it when their ruler devoured them. Later, I learned it was a retelling of Israel's plea for a king in the book of Samuel. *God had warned them, but they wanted one anyway.* Just like I had.

Russell tried to win me back for weeks. He called constantly, his voice a mix of regret and longing, promising change, pleading for another chance. A part of me– tired, lonely, and haunted by the echoes of what we once were– almost believed him. I let myself remember the good moments, the laughter, the softness that occasionally broke through all the chaos.

On Easter Sunday, I agreed to meet him for dinner. The evening was tender, nostalgic in a way that tugged at my heart. Afterward, we ended up at a hotel, and for one night, I let myself fall back into the illusion that maybe love could be rebuilt, that maybe this was our redemption. He had gone out of his way to make it feel right: snacks, movies, a room that smelled faintly of hope and desperation.

For a brief moment, I wanted to believe it too. But the truth came crashing in the instant after I climaxed when the world went still, when the noise inside me quieted, and there was nothing left but clarity. Everything I'd once felt for him, every ounce of affection, every trace of attachment was gone. Completely gone.

What had moments ago felt intimate now felt suffocating, hollow, done. I knew it was over. I asked him to take me home, but he didn't understand. He begged me to stay, his eyes searching mine for something that wasn't there anymore. I filed for divorce soon after. Because I had nothing left for him. Or so I thought.

## CHAPTER 11

# TWO LINES

*Children are a gift from the* LORD; *they are a reward from him. ~Psalm 127:3*

When I became pregnant, I was devastated. Russell and I had been trying for a year, and it happened only after the marriage was over.

Terrified, I called my friend Leila.

"Girl, I missed my cycle," I whispered like I was confessing a crime.

"Don't worry," she said with all the calm of someone who wasn't me. "You're probably just stressed. But I'll get you a pregnancy test."

She worked for a doctor, which meant she had access to things the rest of us only saw locked behind glass at Walgreens. That night, she called: "I got it. Are you coming over?"

Now, did I go that night? No. I decided to be responsible and wait until morning so the results would be "accurate." Like waiting until sunrise was going to make the difference between a baby and no baby. I laid in bed that night, tossing, turning, my bladder screaming for mercy, and still told myself, nope, first thing in the morning.

The next morning before the birds even started their shift I got dressed, grabbed my swollen bladder, and sped over to Leila's. She was already in her room getting ready for work.

"It's in the bathroom," she called out casually, like she had just left me a toothbrush.

So, in I went, closed the door, and sat down on the toilet with that little box in hand. My hands were shaking. My heart was pounding. My bladder was finally rejoicing. I read the instructions three times just to be sure. Then, with all the seriousness of a NASA launch, I did what I had to do.

Before I could even put the cap back on the stick bam! There they were. Two bright pink lines. Instant, bold, and undeniable.

"Oh my God," I whispered. "It's two lines. It's two lines."

Now, listen. I am a woman with a whole vocabulary at my disposal. Degrees. Books read. Life lived. But in that moment, the English language reduced itself to one phrase. I couldn't say I'm pregnant. I couldn't say "Lord, help me." I couldn't even manage "Nooooo!" All I could say, like a broken record stuck on repeat, was:

"It's two lines. It's two lines. It's TWO LINES!"

Leila must've heard the panic in my voice because she knocked.

"Are you okay in there?"

"Two lines," I croaked.

"What?"

"IT'S TWO LINES!"

The door cracked open. She peeked in like I might be dangling from the shower rod. There I was: sitting on the toilet, test in one hand, instruction sheet in the other, my whole world wrecked, chanting the same two words like it was a new gospel.

She snatched the instructions out of my trembling hands, flipping furiously through them like maybe, just maybe, the manufacturer had made a typo. She kept muttering, "What does it say about two lines? What does it say?" as if she could manifest a different outcome by reading it fast enough.

Finally, she stopped, her finger pressed to the little results chart. "Yep. Two lines means positive." She sighed and then, without missing a beat, said the most Leila thing ever:

"You just need to get an abortion and talk it over with Jesus later."

I stared at her. "I can't."

"You can," she insisted.

"I can't," I repeated. "I've already had three. I can't have another one. I just can't."

And there it was, the beginning of my journey with my third child. Not with a prayer. Not with a song. But with me in a bathroom, clutching a pee stick, and repeating the phrase that would echo through my memory forever:

It's two lines.

\*\*\*

I carried that baby with a clenched heart and trembling hands. My prayers were not soft or graceful, they were desperate cries whispered through tears: *"Please, God, make it go away."*

I didn't want the constant reminder of Russell living and breathing inside me. As my child grew, I begged God, *"If I must carry this child, please let it be a girl."*

I was terrified that if it were a boy, he'd inherit his father's face, his receding hairline, his mannerisms, his shadow. But the ultrasound revealed a boy.

From that moment, I sank into a sadness so heavy it became the air I breathed. Each day of that pregnancy felt like a sentence, not a blessing. I didn't want to bring this child into the world because it meant being tied to Russell forever. But I couldn't bring myself to have an abortion either.

My mind was twisted in grief and confusion, and at one point, so warped by hopelessness that I began to believe the only way out was death. If I ended my life, I told myself, I'd take the baby with me, and neither of us would have to endure this pain. No child left without a mother, no child forced to grow up under Russell's influence or, worse, with his family.

In my mind, the plan was simple. I would send my youngest daughter to live with her father. Her older sister was already there in North Carolina, so at least they would be together, safe, loved. That summer, I sent her away believing, in some twisted way, that it would be forever.

By this time, I had stopped going to church. I stopped singing. I stopped everything. The joy that once filled my Sundays had drained out of me completely. But even in my isolation, someone noticed my unraveling. Patrick reached out. He called to check in, made sure I had gas in my car, made sure I wasn't alone.

While I was pregnant with Russell's child, he quietly took care of me. He showed up when no one else did. The same choir director who once got on my nerves for fussing at the alto section was now the one who refused to let me fade away. He saw that I'd stopped coming to rehearsals, stopped showing up to church altogether, and he refused to let me just disappear.

Even my mother, in her own way, tried to help. One morning she burst into my room, flipped on the harsh overhead light, and said firmly, "It's time for this to stop. Get up. Take a shower. Get dressed. Go out. You can't keep lying here."

Something about that moment cracked the fog. Maybe it was her tone, maybe it was love disguised as frustration but it jolted me. I gathered just enough strength to get up, to breathe again, to fight the darkness pressing on my chest. That was when my search began my quest to find someone who could adopt my baby boy, someone who could give him the life I was too broken to offer.

But even as I tried to do the right thing, I was consumed by hatred for the man who had broken me. I despised the fact that I had ever let him touch me, that I had ever loved him, that I had allowed him into my life at all. I wanted to erase every trace of him, every memory, every scar, every echo of his name. I lashed out at anyone who tried to reach me, my words sharp enough to wound, my spirit hardened with regret. I was drowning in disgust, in shame, in the unbearable truth that no matter how hard I tried to forget him, a piece of him was growing inside me, binding me to a man I wanted to forget ever existed.

By the time I was six months pregnant, the world had shifted. The news was everywhere, *the Twin Towers had come down.* The United States had been attacked. Two planes crashed into the World Trade Center, and the sky over New York was on fire. People were running through the streets, covered in ash, screaming, praying, searching for loved ones.

I remember arriving to work to find everyone standing there, frozen, watching the towers collapse live on television. Massive buildings crumbling like sand, disappearing into clouds of smoke that swallowed everything around them. The anchors' voices shook; some could barely speak. No one knew what was happening, only that life as we knew it had just changed.

The Pentagon had been hit. Another plane had gone down in Pennsylvania. Fear and disbelief blanketed the country. Airports around the nation shut down, phone lines jammed, people wept openly in public. For days, the world felt suspended between heartbreak and silence. America was wounded, and we all felt it, whether we were in New York or a thousand miles away.

Working at the Memphis airport as a parts clerk, I was among the first to go: the last one hired, the first one fired. I remember standing in the breakroom, staring at the pink slip, feeling both relief and despair. Relief because I didn't have to paste on a smile anymore, and despair because I had no idea how I would survive with another baby coming.

A different church in Memphis opened its doors to those affected by the layoffs, offering a hundred dollars and a list of resources. That's where I signed up for free therapy. It was there, in that quiet office with a stranger, that I finally admitted the truth out loud: *I didn't want this baby.* I didn't want to be reminded of Russell every time I looked into my child's face.

I prayed that the baby would at least take after me in complexion, that I wouldn't have to see his father staring back at me through innocent eyes. I had already considered sending my daughters away and ending my own life. Adoption seemed like the only way out.

The therapist didn't judge me. She just asked for one thing: a promise. "Wait until the baby is born before you make any decisions," she said softly.

I nodded, though I wasn't sure I could keep that promise.

Three months later, when my water broke on a Saturday morning, panic and numbness collided. I called Patrick, who had been seeing me through those dark months. He drove me to the hospital and stayed by my side. When my son was born, he even cut the umbilical cord. I delivered a healthy baby boy pale, pink, fragile-looking. He resembled, to my horror, a little white lab rat. I recoiled the moment I saw him. I didn't want to hold him, I didn't want to love him, I only wanted to look, to see if there was any trace of Russell in his face.

They took him away, and later, when I was alone in my hospital room, a social worker came in to handle the paperwork for the birth certificate and Social Security number. I wanted to give my son my maiden name, but they wouldn't allow it. He had to carry Russell's name. That broke me. It was like a final act of surrender to a man I despised. When she left, I called the nurses' station, not because I felt maternal, but because I needed to see my baby's ears. I wanted to know if there was any hope that his skin might darken, that he might take after me.

The nurse brought him in, swaddled, in a clear bassinet. I didn't touch him. I didn't whisper to him. I just stared at his ears, pink, soft, and fair with no trace of brown pigment. Defeated, hollow, I wondered, *What am I going to do with this baby that I don't want?*

Then he began to struggle. His tiny chest pulled in and out like breathing was too much work. I pressed the call button and said flatly, "There's something wrong with this baby." The nurse arrived quickly, took one look, and whisked him away to the neonatal intensive care unit (NICU).

The pediatrician returned later, explaining that his lungs were underdeveloped and he'd need to stay overnight for observation. She offered to let me stay with him, but I shook my head. "I can't," I said, my voice cold, distant. "I have two other children at home. It's three days before Christmas. I don't have time for this."

They discharged me that afternoon. But before I left, something tugged at my conscience. I didn't want anyone, especially God, to think I was completely heartless. So, I went to see him.

The NICU was quiet except for the rhythmic hum of machines, the faint antiseptic smell hanging heavy in the air. Rows of babies lay beneath webs of tubes and wires, their skin translucent, their bodies impossibly small. I walked past each incubator until I reached the back of the room, where my full-term baby lay alone with no tubes, no machines, no reason.

Though I refused to nurse him, I couldn't bear the thought of him drinking formula, so I came back to the hospital every day to pump breast milk. Each time I visited, it seemed something new went wrong: first his breathing, then his temperature, then a feeding issue. Every test came back normal. When jaundice set in, they placed him under the blue phototherapy lights. He lay there in nothing but a diaper, his eyes covered, his skin glowing a ghostly blue, fragile and breakable.

I stood there staring down at him, numb, wishing I could will the whole situation away. Then, in the middle of that sterile hum and my spiraling thoughts, a voice cut through the noise clear, sharp, unmistakable. It wasn't my imagination. It was the Holy Spirit: *"You know you are all he has."*

The words pierced straight through the wall I had built around my heart. Something inside me shifted and snapped and in that instant, I knew. I asked the nurse to swaddle him and place him in my arms. That night, I nursed him for the first time, not out of obligation, but out of something deeper, something that finally felt like love.

By morning, the doctor came in smiling. "He's doing better," she said. "He's strong enough to go home." And standing there in that NICU, holding him against my chest, I realized the unthinkable truth: *I* was what was wrong with him.

\*\*\*

When my son was two, my mother gave Russell my phone number. I didn't realize it at the time, but that one decision would reopen a wound I had worked so hard to heal. Foolishly, I allowed Russell to visit with our son. I told myself it was the right thing to do, that maybe my son deserved to know his father, even if I still carried the pain of all he'd done.

One afternoon, after my little boy returned from a visit at Russell's house, I was bathing him when I noticed the bruises, blue, uneven marks scattered across his small backside. My stomach dropped, and a sick, hollow fear filled my chest. My hands froze in the water. For a moment, I couldn't even breathe. Then panic took over, and I grabbed the phone. I called Russell immediately, but the call went straight to voicemail. I called again and again, each attempt ringing into silence until finally, the line disconnected completely.

My fear turned into rage, rage for what he might have done and rage at myself for ever letting him close to our child. I don't know why I called my mother, except that I was angry with her for giving him my number. I knew she didn't care, she never had, never offered any comfort or protection. Still, I called, desperate for some support, and instead of solace, she offered cold justification. "He probably just disciplined him," she said flatly. "The boy must've done something he shouldn't have."

Her words sliced through me. I couldn't believe what I was hearing. I had expected protection, compassion, something. But she gave me none. She sided with him. The man who had broken me, hurt me, and now, I feared, had hurt my child. I was furious with her not just for what she said, but for what it revealed: that she would rather defend him than stand with me. But that was no surprise.

After that day, Russell disappeared. I never heard from him again, not a call, not a letter, nothing for eight long years. Then, one day, when my son was old enough to ask about the father he'd never known. He came to me for answers.

I reached out, and when I finally heard Russell's voice, it was hollow, weary like a man whose choices had drained every ounce of life from him. He told me he was "broken," that he needed to see his son. Against my better judgment, I let them reconnect, just for a while. But it didn't last. The same old pattern repeated. Before long, Russell vanished again, back into the darkness back to prison, where he remains to this day.

The child I once prayed would go away, the baby I begged God not to let live is still here. Still mine, and I love them more than I can ever explain. Because even in my rebellion, even in my brokenness, God kept His promise: *"I will never leave you nor forsake you."*

## CHAPTER 12

# REVERSE DESTRUCTION

*"So, they impaled Haman on the pole he had set up for Mordecai." ~**Esther 7:10a***

Although I was still legally married to Russell, by the time my baby was born, Patrick and I were in a full-blown relationship. But once I had given birth, once I found my strength again, I was ready to move on. But I felt indebted to him, so I stayed, uncommitted. The truth was, I was living a double life, entangled in a relationship with yet another *married* man, constantly chasing validation that always seemed just out of reach.

Two months after my baby's arrival, I enlisted in the Tennessee Army National Guard, spending one weekend each month in Nashville for drill. Patrick sometimes came with me, sometimes he didn't. Our relationship mirrored the pattern of my early entanglement with Ellis: a cycle of breaking up and getting back together, over and over. During one of those "on-again" moments, we conceived.

As the pregnancy progressed the constant monthly commutes eventually became too much to bear, and I made the decision to move to Nashville permanently. I told Patrick I was moving and he could come if he wanted, secretly hoping the negative, and in November 2002, I relocated to Smyrna, Tennessee, with my newborn, my youngest daughter and pregnant with Patrick's baby. Just a week later, he followed.

The next month, I finalized my divorce from Russell. Pregnant and desperate for stability, I took any work I could find: inventory counting, temporary National Guard assignments, anything to keep us afloat. Patrick worked intermittently, but nothing stable. He was constantly traveling back and forth to Memphis seeming unsure that he wanted to stay. Although, when I met him, he told me that it was his house and his mother lived with him, I soon realized he had never truly maintained a household and he was actually living with her. He didn't know how to establish utilities, pay bills, or manage the responsibilities of adult life. It all became clear when he moved in permanently.

After Jeremiah, our son, was born, I found steady work first at a shipping company, then at Verizon Wireless, where I stayed for seven years. With the help of my cousin's husband, who was a manager at a factory, Patrick secured a job there. But despite my efforts and my hope for something lasting, my marriage to Patrick, like every relationship before it, was doomed from the start.

We married on February 12, 2004. On my cousin's advice, I made sure to purchase a house in my name only the day before. Thank God I did. Because once the vows were spoken, Patrick began to chip away at me, piece by piece.

He all but stopped going to work and started using threats as weapons; telling me he'd take our son and leave anytime I didn't bend to his demands. He contributed nothing to the household. His car had already been repossessed before we even left the apartment we'd been living in, which meant we were down to just my vehicle for a long time.

During that period, he always insisted on driving me to work, not out of love or concern, but so he could have access to my car. He would drive it at night because he worked nights, and I used it during the day.

When we needed childcare, because his work hours no longer allowed him to keep our son during the day, he didn't lift a finger to help find anyone. He left it all on me. Through it all, he had this small toiletry-style bag that he carried everywhere like a secret companion. He never let me see what was inside. To this day, I still don't know what all he kept in that bag. Every night he'd come home, take it straight to the bathroom, shower, and then hide it away again until the next day.

One day, by some small stroke of luck, I managed to get a peek inside. My heart sank when I found a pawnshop receipt for a radio someone had given me several years earlier as a Christmas gift. Every time I'd asked him about that radio, he'd told me he had taken it to work but kept forgetting to bring it home. The truth was he had pawned it and he never went back to get it.

Before long, he stopped going to work altogether. Night after night, he'd come home with excuses "they didn't have enough work," "they didn't need as many workers," "they sent people home early." But deep down, I knew something wasn't right. Eventually, I asked my cousin what was up. He said that Patrick either wasn't showing up, was late when he did, or refused to do certain tasks.

After several months of that, they terminated him. And somehow, it was all my fault. He blamed me and said he lost his job because I didn't give him gas money.

Our financial situation crumbled. I was desperate. I had to take out a payday loan just to afford childcare for Jeremiah. When Patrick found the payday loan paperwork in the car, he exploded. He screamed at me for not telling him I'd done it. Of course, I yelled back. We ended up in a heated argument about money, work, childcare and everything that had been building between us.

I tried to walk away, to put distance between us, but he followed me from room to room. I went downstairs to the guest room he followed. I went back upstairs and he followed again. Finally, when I went downstairs a second time, desperate to get away, I grabbed a broomstick and told him to leave me alone. I warned him but he kept coming toward me. When he got close enough, I hit him on the legs with the broomstick, hoping he'd stop. But he didn't.

When I realized it wasn't helping, I dropped the broomstick, ran into the room, and tried to lock the door. He forced it open, came inside, and shut it behind him. I got into the bed, then got up again, pacing, trying to keep calm, trying to get him to just leave me alone. He refused.

When I tried to leave the room, he held the door closed so I couldn't get out. I tried to pry his arm away, and when I finally did, I ran upstairs again. He followed. I ran back downstairs, slammed the door, and managed to lock it. Exhausted, I crawled into bed, hoping to fall asleep to forget him, forget the fight, forget everything. But not before making the worst mistake I could've ever made. In frustration, I said, *"If you don't leave me alone, I'll call the police and tell them you hit me."* It was a bluff, a desperate plea for him to leave me alone. But those words became his weapon.

Thirty minutes later, there was a knock at the door. When I opened it, I was met by the Smyrna Police Department. They told me they'd received a complaint of domestic violence. Patrick had called the police claiming that I had beat him. He told them he didn't want me to go to jail and he would not let them examine him. He just wanted them to talk to me and make me understand that he didn't have money because he had to send it back to Memphis to take care of his mother, and he couldn't work because of all that pressure.

I told the officers what had happened but I left out the part about the broomstick. It didn't matter. I learned that night that in the state of Tennessee, if you touch someone during an argument, it's considered assault. And so, in the home I had bought with my own name on the deed, they handcuffed me, led me out, and arrested me for domestic assault. From that moment on, he used the legal system as a tool for revenge.

On the way to the police station, one of the officers explained that they didn't believe Patrick's story and that the only reason they arrested me was because I had admitted to touching him during the argument. Still, it didn't matter. I was booked, processed, and humiliated. The only small mercy was being released on my own recognizance, and only because I had found somewhere else to stay.

My neighbor down the street, whose daughter was friends with mine, opened her home to me. When I was released, the officer told me I couldn't go home for twelve hours, a so-called "cooling off" period. I counted the hours until I could return, and when the time was up, I walked back into my home as if stepping into a stranger's house.

Patrick acted like nothing had happened. He wanted to be intimate, as though the police, and the humiliation had never taken place. But I couldn't. I didn't want to look at him, touch him, or hear his voice. He understood that now the power had shifted; he was the "victim," and any misstep on my part could send me straight back to jail. Another weapon in his arsenal.

"I'll call the police," he'd say. "I'll tell them you did something." And when that didn't terrify me enough, he'd add, "I'll take our son and move back to Memphis."

Eventually, I grew tired of living under constant threat. So, I devised a plan. Pretending I wanted to seek counsel from his family, I suggested a trip to Memphis. As we neared his mother's house, I asked him to stop at Kmart to pick something up for me. The moment he stepped inside, my heart pounding in my chest, I slid into the driver's seat and took off heading back to Smyrna, leaving him in Memphis, making good on his threat.

It didn't take long before my phone rang. His voice came through like a storm. "What are you doing?" he shouted.

I told him calmly, "You keep saying you'll take our son and go back to Memphis. Well, here you are."

His response froze the blood in my veins: "I am going to utterly destroy you."

The very next day, his brother-in-law drove him back to Smyrna. Because we were married, the police said I had to let him in. One of the officers warned me bluntly, "If we have to come back here, ma'am you're going to jail." That was my breaking point. I gathered my children and a few belongings and went back to my neighbor's house, waiting for Monday morning so I could file for divorce.

While I was staying at my neighbor's house, he filed the first of more than twenty Department of Children's Service (DCS) reports of alleged child abuse and neglect against me. He told them that our son was sick and that I was refusing to give him his medication. The truth was far from that. I had simply called and asked if he could pick up our son's prescription from the pharmacy because I didn't have the money at the time, and I didn't want to drag the children out just for that one errand.

But Patrick twisted my words into a weapon. Every conversation, every small request, became ammunition for his cruelty, a new reason to cause me pain, to make me appear unfit, to keep me trapped in his web of control. What began as a plea for help became the first shot in a relentless campaign to destroy me.

Patrick stayed in my home, determined to torment me from within those walls. It rained all weekend, and just to spite me, he turned on the water hose and let the water run nonstop to run up the bill, to make sure I paid for every drop.

On Monday morning, I took the day off to find an attorney. I managed to secure one to begin the divorce process and went into work, hoping things might finally begin to shift. But that afternoon, my neighbor's husband called in a panic. "He's got a U-Haul backed up to your garage," he said. "He's moving all the furniture out of the house."

I rushed home again and called the police. They told him he couldn't remove any of the furniture, so he begrudgingly returned the truck but his retaliation was swift. When that plan failed, he filed an order of protection against me. In it, he even included our children, claiming I was unfit to be near them. But once the reality set in that he would be solely responsible for their care, their meals, their child care, their every need he quickly had them removed from the order.

But the cruelty didn't stop there. He began calling my friends, telling them he wanted to reconcile, that he just wanted to talk, pretending to seek peace. What I didn't know was that he was setting a trap. His real plan was to lure me into meeting with him so he could accuse me of violating an order of protection I didn't even know existed. But I refused.

Later that week, we went to court to begin the divorce process. In the paperwork, the judge made it clear that neither of us was allowed to sell or dispose of any property. So, Patrick, although I am not sure how, returned to Memphis. Once he got there, he filed yet another order of protection against me this time claiming that I had called and threatened his life. Of course, he couldn't produce a single phone record to support his accusation.

My attorney and I drove all the way to Memphis so I could appear in court. When we arrived, the judge sternly warned that any retaliatory orders of protection would be denied, and that anyone filing one out of spite could face jail time. At that point, Patrick quickly dropped the case.

One afternoon, while I was at work taking calls at Verizon Wireless, a supervisor approached my desk and told me I needed to come to the front of the building. When I stepped into the lobby, a sheriff's deputy was waiting for me. Her face was unreadable, official. She handed me a folded stack of papers, an *ex parte* order of protection and began explaining its terms. I wasn't to contact Patrick in any way, she said, and I had to sign acknowledging I understood. She signed, dated and time stamped the document, 12:24 PM.

Three days later–on a Thursday–I was called to the front again. I remember feeling confused, my stomach tightening with unease. There stood yet another sheriff's deputy waiting. This time, there was no conversation. He informed me that I was under arrest for violating the order of protection. My mind went blank. I hadn't done anything. I didn't even understand what was happening.

He placed me in handcuffs and led me out of the building, past my coworkers, my heart pounding so hard I could hear it echoing in my ears. At the county jail, I was booked, fingerprinted, and processed.

It turned out that when an order of protection is served, the "victim" is immediately notified and told that the "offender" has been officially served and knows to stay away. The moment Patrick got that call, he struck again. He called the magistrate's office and reported a violation of the order. He said that after that call from the sheriff's department, he had received a call and "someone" in a muffled voice said they were going to kill him. Even though it had only just been served. The warrant for my arrest was signed at 12:54 p.m., barely thirty minutes after I'd received the paperwork.

This time, I couldn't be released on my own recognizance. The only way out was to post bail $500 cash money I didn't have. No one I knew had it either, or wanted to pay it. And honestly, I couldn't blame them. My cousin, seeing the situation for what it was, told me I should stay in jail until my court date on Monday. She was right, because every time I was released, Patrick was notified, and he'd use it to fabricate another accusation.

So, I stayed. Four long, endless days in that cold, concrete cell. Time lost all meaning. The air was heavy with despair, the walls sweating with the echoes of other people's misery. I barely slept, my body too tense, my mind too loud, replaying every moment that had led me there. I ate only because my cellmate insisted, sliding the tray toward me with quiet concern, as if she could see that I was unraveling from the inside out.

Every chance I got; I called my children. They were staying at my cousin's house for the weekend. My cousin was away, so my fifteen-year-old daughter had to shoulder a burden no child should ever carry. She was forced to parent my two toddlers, to feed them, comfort them, and keep them safe, while I sat trapped behind bars, paying for the cruelty of a man consumed by vengeance, his wrath spilling over onto me, onto my children, onto everyone in his path.

The metal bench beneath me became my bed, hard and unforgiving. Every inch of my body ached from it. The fluorescent lights never went dark; they buzzed incessantly, drilling through every thought, every prayer, every fragile attempt at peace.

Each night, an announcement would echo through the intercom cold, mechanical, almost inhuman. It was a safety warning for the guards and staff: instructions for where to go, what to do in case of an emergency where *they* could go to be protected. But for us the inmates there was nothing. The voice would always end the same way: *"Inmates are to remain where they are."* I was sure that I was going to die in there. All I could think was: *How had my life come to this?*

When Monday finally came, I was led into the courtroom in an orange jumpsuit, wrists cuffed, feeling exposed and hollow. Patrick was there, sitting like he owned the room. But the moment he saw me in that jumpsuit, his composure cracked. He told the judge he needed to get an attorney.

The judge looked at him, confused. "You're the victim," he said. "Why do you need an attorney?"

Patrick just kept repeating himself. "I need an attorney. I need an attorney."

But I knew why. He was lying. He wasn't panicking. He thought if he stalled long enough, I'd sit in jail even longer.

I couldn't bear another night behind those walls. I scraped together what little money I had, money I couldn't afford to lose and used it to post bond. The next day, we returned to court. This time, I had my attorney with me.

When Patrick saw me walk in, free and standing tall, his face fell. He claimed again that he hadn't been able to find an attorney, another delay tactic. But now the judge had lost his patience. His voice was sharp as he said, "We're not waiting any longer. We're going to stop the bleed on this one today."

He heard the case right then and there and dismissed the order of protection. But before we left the courtroom, Patrick made a careless comment during testimony about filing another report against me. My attorney immediately requested a brief recess. We went upstairs to another courtroom, filed an order of protection *against him,* and had it signed by another judge on the spot.

When we returned to the courtroom below, the papers were served to him right then and there in front of the same judge, the same audience, the same system he had used to torment me. In that moment, the tables finally turned. For a little while anyway.

In September of 2004, the same year Patrick and I were married, we were divorced. By November, I finally faced court for the assault charge. My attorney managed to get it reduced to simple assault, a crucial adjustment that allowed me to continue my military career. A domestic assault conviction carries consequences far beyond the courtroom: you cannot carry a weapon, and without that ability, you cannot serve in the United States Armed Forces. Patrick knew this.

For the next twelve years, he made my life a living hell. He called DCS, orchestrated false complaints, and had me arrested not once, not twice, but a total of four times.

When I wouldn't answer his calls, he dispatched police for "wellness checks," turning my life into a constant state of scrutiny and fear. My only recourse, my only defense in court was the fact that he had never voluntarily paid child support. The only money I received from him came from intercepted income tax refunds.

Patrick didn't stop there. He went to my National Guard unit, spreading lies that I had been convicted of domestic assault. He harassed Verizon Wireless, falsely claiming I had accessed his cell phone account without authorization. Their system recorded each access with an identifier, proving that I had done nothing. Yet he continued to call incessantly, prompting Verizon to summon me to HR not for a job interview, as I had expected for a trainer position, I had applied for, but to plead with me to get him to stop. He had begun harassing the company because they refused to fire me.

Court appearances consumed every bit of my leave and sick time. My National Guard unit recognized the harassment, and eventually, I went on active duty as a recruiter, a turning point, as my job at Verizon was at risk due to the frequent absences. I thank God for my incredible supervisor, who protected and supported me through it all, even as Patrick continued to refuse any financial or moral responsibility for our son.

Patrick's tactics were insidious. He repeatedly told Jeremiah that everything I was trying to teach him was wrong. Any rule I set, anything I did that he didn't like, became ammunition for Patrick. Jeremiah was encouraged to report it to him, and Patrick would "handle it." In practice, this meant that Patrick would call the police, file false allegations against me, and demand emergency custody. These accusations were always denied, but the cycle continued, dragging me through the same round of false claims over and over.

Jeremiah's defiance grew more intense, and the confusion he caused began to affect the other children. Even they, at times, began lobbying for him to go live with Patrick. The situation became untenable. In the face of it all, I reached a point where I simply couldn't keep fighting.

I had fought hard. I fought for my children, for my sanity, for my very survival. Every battle was uphill, every small victory hard-won, yet I endured. I survived. Patrick did not destroy me. He destroyed himself.

## CHAPTER 13

# WOMAN AT THE WELL

*"You are right when you say you have no husband. The fact is, you have had five husbands, and the man you now have is not your husband." ~**John 4:17b-18a***

I remember the first time I saw Randall. We served in the same National Guard Battalion, different units, but the same long boring weekends. We had never spoken, not once. Yet, I noticed him. From across the drill floor, in the blur of uniforms and formations, my eyes found him. There was something about him that made me think, if he ever asked me, I'd say yes. Why? I couldn't have told you then. Maybe because, at that time, I was drowning in my own sad loneliness.

I had made a mess of my life and it had me by the throat. I was trapped in the relentless grind of trying to make ends meet, take care of my kids, piecing together some sense of worth when I barely believed I had any left. Patrick's revenge machine was in full force. I was angry, exhausted, and utterly alone. Maybe that's all it would've taken just one person, somebody, anybody to see me, to ask for me, and I would have said yes.

One night during an overnight weekend drill, I was lying on the bottom bunk in the barracks, listening to music, when my phone rang.

"*Hello?*"

"*Hey girl, what you doing?*" It was Teresa, a friend from another unit.

"*Nothing,*" I said. "*Just laying here.*"

"*Hold on,*" she said.

A new voice came through the line. Deep. Confident. "*Get your ass up and come outside.*"

"*What? Who is this?*" I asked.

He said his last name, and I knew immediately. It was Randall.

Fifteen minutes later, I was dressed and outside, climbing into his car. Teresa and her boyfriend were in the backseat; Randall was behind the wheel. I slipped into the passenger seat like I'd been meant to be there all along. The night air felt electric, alive. For the first time in a long time, I felt wanted. Desired. Chosen.

We bought some alcohol and went back to one of the rooms in the barracks. For the next hour, we laughed, listened to music, played cards, and just talked. It felt easy. Familiar. The world outside that little room didn't exist for a while. When Teresa and her boyfriend curled up on one bunk, it seemed only natural that Randall and I lay on the other.

He wrapped his arms around me, and for the first time in so long, I felt safe. I felt… loved. In that moment, everything else faded, the weight of my life, the chaos waiting for me back home, the ache of loneliness it felt I had been lugging around my entire life.

For that brief, stolen hour, I allowed myself to believe that maybe I was worthy of something gentle. Something real. But, of course, there was a catch. There was always a catch.

Randall was married.

\*\*\*

A few months later, our unit deployed to Mississippi for a dreaded two-week field training exercise, what the National Guard officially calls "annual training." The days were long, the air was thick with humidity, and the nights buzzed with mosquitoes and fatigue.

I drove my van down to Mississippi with two other female soldiers. When we arrived, we were assigned our barracks, if you could even call them that. They looked like something out of a horror movie. Dust and cobwebs hung like curtains, the mattresses looked older than some of the soldiers, and the air smelled faintly of mildew and regret. But in true military fashion, we adapted.

We grabbed our wallets, drove straight to Walmart, and stocked up on everything: plastic mattress covers, cleaning supplies, and bug spray, lots of bug spray. By the time we were done scrubbing and decorating, that old barracks looked halfway livable, almost cozy. But not really.

During our downtime, we made the best of it. We'd pile into whichever car had the most seats and head into the nearby college town, sometimes to a local restaurant, sometimes to a place called *The Library*. Don't let the name fool you, it wasn't where you went to study. It was a bar, disguised cleverly enough that the students could say with a straight face, "I'm going to The Library," and not technically be lying.

The following weekend was Father's Day. Patrick, for once, was being decent and had visitation with my sons, who were only two and three at the time. I drove to Memphis to visit them and help them celebrate with him. It was bittersweet, watching my boys laugh while knowing how broken everything else was, but I was grateful just to see them smile.

When I got back to Mississippi on Sunday afternoon, before our accountability formation, I decided I didn't want to have dinner alone. Scrolling through my phone, I landed on Randall's name purely by accident, his last name started with "A," so he was first in my contacts list. I smiled to myself and hit the call button.

He picked up, and before long we were sitting across from each other at a local buffet, laughing between bites of steak, the best steak I'd ever eaten in my entire life. "In all my thirty-eight years, I've never had steak that tasted this good." I proclaimed.

Maybe it was the seasoning, maybe it was the company, or maybe it was just the first time in a long while that dinner felt easy. I grinned at him and said, "You know, you should feel lucky you're having dinner with me. I only called you because your name came up first in my phone."

He laughed, leaning back in his chair. "Oh, so this isn't about me, you just scrolled to the top and settled, huh?"

I grinned. "Exactly." I said, taking another bite.

He shook his head, smiling that slow, charming smile. "Well, I'll take luck over nothing." He was incredibly charming.

That dinner changed everything. After that, we were inseparable, moving around like a couple even though we both knew we weren't one. We ate dinner together, played cards late into the night, went to the drive-in, shared inside jokes. I knew what it was.

I wasn't special. I wasn't the exception. He wasn't looking for love, he was looking for a hookup. Even knowing that, I stayed. I told myself I could handle it, that I just wanted the company, but deep down, I wanted to believe him when he said he felt trapped and broken in his marriage.

When it was time to head home, the two soldiers I'd driven down with had to leave early, which left me with an empty passenger seat. Randall, who had rode with the unit, filled it without hesitation.

Randall drove my van for five hours, talking to me the entire way, weaving his pain into words that made me feel like I was his salvation. He told me how much he hated his marriage, how broken he felt, how he wished things were different. When I told him I had been married and divorced five times, he asked me if I would ever get married again. I laughed; told him no one would ever want to marry someone like me.

"You don't know that." His eyes met mine momentarily as he spoke.

We'd stayed up nearly all night before the drive, and by the time we reached my house, we were both exhausted. He helped me bring in my bags, and without thinking, we collapsed on my bed and fell asleep. The next day, he called and asked me to dinner. Just like that, we slipped into something neither of us could name, and neither of us could walk away from.

We talked every night, stole every moment we could. Then, his wife found out. She went through his phone. She saw my number, saw how often we talked, the pattern that had formed, the hours and days that traced the outline of our affair.

She called me and left a voicemail while I was in class. Her voice was calm and simmering with fury. I was in training in Little Rock, Arkansas at the time, and couldn't take calls during the day. But before I could even think of what to say, she called again. And again. And again. Four times in a single day. Each message was soaked in anger, betrayal, and disbelief, her voice breaking between rage and heartbreak.

I never answered. I never called her back.

That should have been the moment I walked away. That should have been the moment I faced the truth, that this thing I was clinging to was not love. It was destruction. It was theft, not just of her husband, but of peace, hers, mine, and our children's. But instead of walking away, her anger lit something ugly inside me. It became a challenge.

In one of her voicemails, she said, *"This is Mrs. Randall Anderson. A title you will never hold."*

Those words echoed in me like a dare. My pride rose up, wounded and stubborn. My brokenness clung to that sentence like a battle cry. I wanted to prove her wrong, to take what she had, to show her that I could, and I did.

What followed was war. A war of restraining orders, voicemails, harassment, and arrests. She called my house, screamed through the phone, cursed at my children. She fought tooth and nail for a man who was already gone. Randall, he played the victim on both sides. He never defended me, never defended her. He just stood there, silent and cowardly, letting two women destroy each other over someone who wasn't worth the time of day.

All the while, I was still in court battles with Patrick. Still fighting for custody of my son. Still trying to keep my life from collapsing completely.

While he and his wife were still legally married, he left her and moved in with me. He said she'd filed for divorce, though I never saw the papers. But that didn't stop me from clinging to the illusion that we were building something real. I don't know if I was embarrassed, prideful, or just lost, (all of the above) but I refused to let go of something that had never been mine to take.

In the end, she took almost everything from him. When he retired from the military, she got half of his retirement pay. He was ordered to pay child support for their four sons, all under fifteen, plus their insurance, medical expenses, everything. And me, in all my foolishness, said, "It doesn't matter. She's alone now. We have each other."

But we didn't. Not really.

The truth was, I didn't even want him. I didn't need him. What I wanted was to win. To prove something, to her, to him, maybe even to myself. I wanted to be Mrs. Randall Anderson, not because I loved him, but because I refused to lose.

Even after their divorce, their battle never ended. She controlled when he saw his children, poisoned every exchange, and sent them to our home with instructions to disrespect me. And I endured it. I stayed. Because after everything, the fights, the shame, the damage, I'd invested too much to walk away. I told myself that leaving would mean I'd wasted it all. That walking away would make me nothing.

What I couldn't see, what I refused to see, was that I already was nothing to him. I had fought, clawed, and destroyed pieces of myself and others for a man who never chose me. A man who was never mine to begin with. But I was determined. Sadly, it was like a real-life depiction of the scene from the movie *The Family That Preys*, where Sanaa Lathan's character tells her mother (Alfre Woodard) that she is going to enjoy the ride on the way (to disaster).

He spent our entire marriage trying to get revenge on his ex-wife. Every dollar went to attorneys, every argument was about her, every choice was a way to fight a battle he had already lost. He lost his car, borrowed countless amounts of money from his mother, and I was left carrying the weight of a man who didn't know how to let go of his past.

Even my teenage daughters saw it. They told me I was wrong, that I had no business being with this man. But I didn't listen. I convinced myself this was my last chance at marriage, at love, at being wanted. And so, I stayed. I pushed and pushed until he married me.

And when he did, I reached out to her. I called his ex-wife just to say, "I'm Mrs. Randall Anderson now." I wanted her to feel the same sting of pain I had felt. But how absurd; Randall was her husband! My so-called righteous indignation should have humbled me, but instead, I was consumed by selfish arrogance, too blind to see the truth.

The marriage was a disaster. His money management skills were worse than mine, and that was saying something. He allowed his children to treat me and my children with blatant disrespect, and I never could have imagined that he would one day betray me with infidelity. Duh!

Little by little, I began to see how he sabotaged everything we tried to build together. Every time we sat down to make plans, he would agree in the moment, only to rise from that table and do the exact opposite of what he had committed to. It was as though destruction was his default.

Passive-aggressive was his watch word. Even worse, he carried a deep, quiet jealousy toward me. Any step I took toward success, any small accomplishment I tried to celebrate, he resented. Rather than cheering me on, he seemed to despise the very idea of me thriving.

*\*\*\**

My mother died a few months after we married. When she passed, it felt as though I had finally been released from a prison I hadn't even realized I'd lived in my entire life. For so long, I'd been bound by her voice, her expectations, her criticism. I had spent years walking on eggshells, terrified that every word, every choice, every mistake would find its way back to her, that she would call me, berate me, remind me that I was stupid, that I was never enough. But suddenly, that voice was gone. The echo that had haunted me since childhood went silent.

It was over. Finally, mercifully, over.

For the first time, I didn't have to be perfect. I didn't have to perform or prove or pretend. I no longer had to chase a love that was never coming. I was free, free from her control, free from the weight of her judgment, free from the endless cycle of trying to earn the affection she was incapable of giving.

In 1984, Deniece Williams released a song called *"Black Butterfly."* In it, she sings:

*Black butterfly, sail across the waters,*
*Tell your sons and daughters*

*What the struggle brings.*
*Black butterfly, set the skies on fire,*
*Rise up even higher*
*So the ageless winds of time can catch your wings.*

When I graduated from high school in the same year, I remember driving with the windows down, singing *"Black Butterfly"* at the top of my lungs, believing with all my heart that I was finally going to fly away from all the drama and pain that had filled my life up to that point. I thought freedom was just beyond the horizon, that if I could just keep going, I'd soar.

But the truth was, I was never free. My leg was chained, like a bird tethered inside its own cage. I flapped and fluttered and dreamed of open skies, but the chain kept me bound to the same pain, the same cycle, the same need to prove my worth.

It wasn't until she died that I finally felt the weight of that chain fall away. For the first time, I could breathe. I could *feel* the air beneath my wings. I was free, not just from her, but from the prison of needing her love, her approval, her acceptance. I was free in my body, in my mind, in my spirit.

When the noise of the world finally quieted, when the chaos and striving faded into silence, I began to see everything clearly for what it truly was. I realized I wasn't supposed to be here, not in this place, not in this marriage. None of it was ever meant to be.

That was the moment I understood the truth I had been too afraid to face: I had wrecked my life, and my children's lives, for a man who had never loved me, and never would.

But I stayed. I wrestled with myself, with God, with the very calling on my life. The spiritual warfare was relentless. Every day felt like a battle on the inside, a tug-of-war between what my heart knew was right and the chains of pride and control that told me I had to endure. I had been married too many times to walk away, and yet, God whispered, over and over, that this was not His will.

Probably the only good that came from this marriage was the church we attended, a church I still attend to this day. Even amid the chaos, the deceit, the madness I had stepped into, I clung to holiness in the smallest ways I could. I told myself a thousand lies to justify staying: that Randall's marriage was already over before ours began, that if we asked for forgiveness, it would make everything right, that somehow, if we remained, God would bless it. *"Stupid, stupid, stupid."* I could hear my mother say.

Yet, in all of it, I insisted on one thing: we had to go to church somewhere. In all the years, through all the turmoil, the only decision Randall seemed firm about was the church we would attend. Mount Zion Baptist Church in Nashville. I later learned his ex-wife went there as well.

Thank God, there was never drama, never confrontation. I never saw her there while we were married. But I didn't want to go. In my opinion, it was too large, too impersonal, a pastor who wouldn't know us. Perhaps that was exactly why it was the right place. Bishop Joseph Warren Walker, III is, without question, the most anointed man I have ever met, and he has a memory like an elephant.

Every sermon he delivered struck my heart like fire. Since joining in May 2009, I can count on one hand the sermons that didn't penetrate me, almost every single sermon cut me to the bone. It was as if God Himself was speaking directly to me through that man, reminding me, pleading with me, warning me over and over that what I was doing was wrong. I could not escape it, could not silence it.

For eight long years, I wrestled with Randall, with the lies, with the infidelity, with the passive-aggressive manipulations, and most of all, with God. Then, one sermon on New Year's Eve 2014, though I cannot remember the title, or recall the exact message, pierced me with clarity. *"Get out of Egypt,"* he said.

That was the moment God made it undeniable. I knew I had to leave. But even then, I stayed. Another whole year. I moved out twice, and each time, Randall followed, not out of love, but because he had nowhere else to go. Every day, the battle raged within me: the tug-of-war between fear and freedom, between obligation and obedience, between earthly chains and divine truth. The spiritual warfare was brutal, exhausting, and relentless, but it was in that war that I finally began to glimpse the freedom God had been calling me to all along.

Randall finally left only when there was another woman waiting for him. She told him she wouldn't be with him unless he had divorce papers, and so, he signed them. Just like that, it was over. Just like that, I was free.

But was I?

Freedom felt like an illusion. Though the papers said I was released, my soul was still shackled. I had become a prisoner of my own bad decisions, a captive of my own control. For so long, I had determined that I would be a wife and a mother, that I would have the love, the life, and the stability I believed I deserved, no matter the cost. Even if it meant sacrificing myself. Even if it meant wounding others.

Somewhere along the way, I lost myself in that pursuit. I had become the woman at the well in John chapter four, but truthfully, I was even lower than that. More like the woman at the *bottom* of the well. If John 4:7 had been written about me, it might have read something like this:

*"When Jesus sat down at the well, He heard a voice echoing up from deep within its darkness,*

*'Help me... help me. I have fallen and I can't get out. I am a fool, and I don't know which way to turn.'"*

That was me, calling out from the depths of my own making. I was humiliated, ashamed, and weighted by the consequences of choices that brought me no benefit at all. Just as Romans 6:21 says, *"What benefit did you reap at that time from the things you are now ashamed of?"* I had gained nothing but the shame of years of bad decisions, and the bitter awareness that I had traded my entire life for an illusion.

## CHAPTER 14

# STEPPING INTO THE LIGHT

*"For we are God's handiwork, created in Christ Jesus to do good works, which God prepared in advance for us to do." ~Ephesians 2:10*

Randall and I divorced in May 2016. We were together for a total of eleven years. Whenever I think about it, I'm always reminded of that 1995 Mary J Blige hit *Not Gon' Cry* when she says:

*Eleven years out of my life*
*Besides the kids, I have nothing to show*
*Wasted my years, a fool of a wife*
*I should have left your ass long time ago*

But it was time for the blaming to stop because I had no one to blame but myself.

It had taken me six marriages, four baby daddies, three abortions, and nearly fifty years of selfish, destructive behavior to finally stop and ask myself some hard questions: *How do you keep finding yourself back here? What is the problem– that you can't seem to maintain a stable life? What, or who, is the common denominator in all this pain? And most importantly, what are you going to do about it? What is your plan for change?*

The love and stability I had spent my entire life chasing seemed to slip through my fingers like sand through an hourglass, leaving me empty and alone time and time again. There was no one to blame, only me.

I call 2016 the year of my *valley experience*, the year I walked through the valley of the shadow of death. Randall had moved in with his new girlfriend, changing women like he changed underwear.

His ex-wife launched a full campaign of torment against me. She flooded my DMs with message after hateful message, left cruel voicemails, and seemed to take joy in my misery. Honestly, who could blame her? I was the one who had married her husband out of spite, then rubbed it in her face. Maybe that's why it took me so long to leave, because deep down, I knew I was wrong the entire time. I was too prideful to own it and now I was reaping what I had sown.

Then there was Patrick. For all eleven years, I was with Randall, Patrick harassed me relentlessly, trying again and again to take custody of Jeremiah. At least four times, he dragged me back to court. During one of those hearings, something about him caught my attention. As he sat on the witness stand, his body angled sideways, his voice distorted and barely rising above a whisper. Each time we appeared in court, it was the same, his posture guarded, his face turned away, as if he were hiding something.

Then he began wearing a mask. This was long before COVID made it common. Patrick wore that mask everywhere, and I couldn't help but wonder why.

It wasn't until much later that I learned the truth. He had developed cancer, something that had ravaged his face and left him needing reconstructive surgery and a facial prosthesis. The disease had disfigured him so deeply that he never went without that mask again.

It was then that I truly understood the weight of God's words: *"Vengeance is mine, says the Lord; I will repay."*

Seeing him like that broke my heart. No matter what we had endured, I had never wished him harm. I remembered a moment years earlier when I had cried out to God, pleading for justice, asking why Patrick could keep getting away with filing false charges against me. I wanted him to face consequences and go to jail, just once.

In that still, small voice, God had answered, *"What if he can't handle jail, Jené? What if he goes to jail, and it's too much, and he takes his own life? Could you live with that?"*

I had wept then, apologizing to God for even daring to ask such a question. Watching Patrick hide behind his mask, I realized the truth: I never wanted him to suffer. I had only been angry, hurt and desperate for him to stop trying to take my son. So instead of cursing him, I began to pray for him.

But I didn't stop there. I prayed for Randall. I prayed for his girlfriend. I prayed for his ex-wife. I prayed for everyone I felt had ever wounded me. Not those polite, surface-level prayers either. These were deep, raw, soul-baring prayers, prayers that left me trembling. I poured out my pain, confessed my jealousy, admitted how much it hurt to see Randall move on, how much it stung to watch others find love while I lay alone night after night.

It was some of the deepest pain I had ever known, yet in that pain, I felt God's presence more vividly than ever before, guiding me, holding me, helping me navigate the rocky path I had chosen. I remember praying one specific prayer over and over: *"Lord, show me me... and then show me how to be different. I want to be holy."*

He did. He took me on a journey back through my past, deep into the shadows of who I had been, so I could finally confront the woman I was and discover the woman I was created to be.

Even my home seemed to mirror the darkness I was walking through. It was long and narrow, with few windows to let in the light. The garage was in the back, so I always entered through the rear door, stepping into dimly lit rooms and narrow hallways that seemed to press in on me. Upstairs was no different, small side windows that looked out only to the brick exterior of the neighboring houses, so close you could almost touch them.

So many nights I remember lying there between those cold sheets, crying out to God, begging Him to hold me in His arms. So many days I spent on my knees in my closet, praying, pleading, weeping for Him to take the pain away.

In that darkness, I began to seek light wherever I could find it. I immersed myself in everything that spoke to healing, books on relationships, personal growth, forgiveness, love, faithfulness, and trust. I was deeply troubled by the woman I had become, and I could feel something stirring inside me, a tug on my heart that whispered there was more, that I was meant for more. I *had* to change, because I believed I was created for something greater.

One book in particular, *The Bait of Satan* by John Bevere, opened my eyes. It revealed how the enemy uses the spirit of offense to trap us, to derail us from the purpose God designed us for. I realized how easily I had fallen into that snare, how offense and bitterness had stolen my peace and blurred my focus.

Then came *The Shack* by William P. Young. That story shattered me in the best way possible. It showed me the unimaginable power of forgiveness, how it frees not just others, but your own soul.

I spent countless hours watching YouTube testimonies, soaking in stories of people who had been broken and rebuilt, who, like me, were trying to make sense of their pain. I began to see that these battles we face are never just physical; they are deeply spiritual. Slowly, a veil lifted. I started to recognize the warfare around me, the unseen battle for my peace, my purpose, my very soul.

With that understanding, I finally saw what was happening with Patrick. He wasn't just fighting me; he was fighting a darkness he didn't even recognize. The cancer, the rage, the bitterness, it had all consumed him from the inside out. He became a casualty of the same spiritual war I was learning to fight.

By this time, I was worn down, emotionally drained, hollowed out, and too tired to fight anymore. The custody battles had stripped me of every ounce of strength I had left. I found myself having a quiet, broken conversation with God, the kind that comes not from words but from tears. Once again, I prayed for the attacks to stop. The weight of it all felt unbearable.

I had just come through my sixth divorce, and I was deep in the valley, my season of utter despair. When God asked me what I wanted, my voice trembled with exhaustion as I whispered, *"I'm tired. I just want to give up custody. I can't fight anymore."*

But even as the words left my mouth, my heart ached. The thought of my son being hurt tore through me. I knew Patrick didn't truly care about him, this wasn't about love or concern. It was about control, about punishing me and making my life harder in every way he could. I feared what might happen to Jeremiah in his care, but I was too broken to keep resisting.

Then came God's gentle response, a whisper that seemed to quiet every storm inside me: *"Don't worry. I will take care of it. I will take care of him."*

Those words settled over me like a soft blanket of peace. I didn't understand how He would do it, but I chose to believe Him, and so, with a heart heavy enough to crush me, I made the hardest decision of my life. I agreed to let him go.

I sat down and wrote a parenting plan granting Patrick full custody. Jeremiah was thirteen at the time, and it felt like I was signing away a piece of my own soul. But even as I signed, I clung to God's promise, that He would watch over my boy, even when I couldn't.

It was the hardest act of surrender I had ever made. But in that valley of exhaustion, I learned what true trust in God meant. I had to believe that when I couldn't hold my son, God's arms would. Jeremiah wanted it. He had asked to go.

Even after Patrick gained custody, the torment continued. He continued to make things difficult, obstructing visitation and stirring up chaos just to keep me in pain. Yet, despite having what he claimed to want, he still didn't treat Jeremiah well. That truth broke me all over again.

Just a month after moving in with his father, Jeremiah came back to me and said, *"I shouldn't have left."* Yet, he stayed another year, enduring neglect, and loneliness.

***

My spiritual journey has now led me to a place of revelation, a season where I am awakening to the understanding of my own spiritual gifts: the gift of prophecy, encouragement, and wisdom. These were treasures I had long tried to bury, gifts I once hid out of fear because they had been mocked, dismissed, and misunderstood when I was younger.

The people around me couldn't recognize who I truly was, because they hadn't yet discovered who *they* were.

They couldn't teach me the things I was destined to learn for myself, truths I had been uniquely created to uncover and share with the world. It was in the depths of my darkest valley that I finally began to grasp the fullness of God's love, and in doing so, I learned how to truly love myself.

I won't sugarcoat it; life was still a struggle. Especially financially. I had never truly learned how to manage money. For years, I was just barely keeping my household afloat. It always felt like I was juggling too many balls at once, robbing Peter to pay Paul, doing whatever it took just to make it to the next paycheck. But even in the chaos, I kept pressing on. I was determined to learn, to grow, to figure things out.

Desperate to keep my head above water, I drove for Uber, borrowed money from my sister, and did everything I could to stay afloat. When Randall failed to pay the car note, I had to take the vehicle from him, another weight added to shoulders that already felt like they were carrying the world.

Deep inside, I knew what I needed to do. The Holy Spirit had been whispering it to me for months: *"File for bankruptcy."* But I resisted. I didn't want to. I told myself it was irresponsible, that it meant failure. I kept insisting that if I could just work harder, just pay one more bill, just find one more way, I could fix it myself. I was still trying to control what only God could handle.

For more than a year, I had been waiting on a check from the Department of Veterans Affairs for $2,500. It wasn't much, but to me it meant hope. It meant catching up. It meant finally being able to breathe again. But the money never came.

Then, one day, something inside me broke, not in defeat, but in surrender. I finally decided to obey. I filed for bankruptcy, choosing to trust God instead of my own understanding.

And on *that very same day*, the check was deposited into my account.

I couldn't believe it. It was as though God had been waiting for me to let go, to trust Him completely, to take my hands off what He wanted to fix. That day, I understood something profound: obedience unlocks blessings.

I remembered standing in church not long before that moment, praying for clarity, for a sign, for some direction. A woman at the altar looked at me and said, *"Whatever He tells you to do, do it."* Her words stayed with me. When I finally did, everything began to shift.

A month later, I moved.

I left behind that dark, suffocating house, the one that seemed to mirror all the heaviness I had been living under. I stepped into a new home, one filled with light. Windows in every room. Sunlight streamed through every corner, warming the air around me.

It felt like I had finally emerged from the valley, from the shadows of despair into the glow of renewal. For the first time in years, I could breathe deeply, freely. It wasn't just a new home. It was a new beginning. A new chapter. It was February 2017.

As the light poured through those windows, I knew: God had been faithful all along. He had been waiting for me, not to fight harder, but to finally trust Him enough to rest. But my real transformation wasn't about money or a house. It was about *me*.

That's when I discovered the power of affirmations, the art of speaking life over myself. I began to stand in front of the mirror, staring into the eyes of a woman I had spent years longing to love, and I forced myself to say the words: *"I am beautiful."*

At first, the words felt foreign, almost forbidden. Each time they left my lips, I felt a jolt of resistance, as if I were breaking some unspoken rule. I would flinch at the sound of my own voice, whispering truth into a place that had known only shame. But I kept saying it. I kept flinching, until one day, it didn't hurt anymore.

Somewhere along the way, the words sank in. What began as hesitant repetition became a holy declaration. *I am beautiful.* It was no longer just a phrase; it was a truth that rewrote the way I saw myself. My perspective began to shift, and the world around me shifted with it.

When people asked, "How are you?" I stopped answering with the empty, automatic *"I'm fine."* Instead, I smiled and said, *"I'm beautiful, thank you for asking."*

That's when something remarkable happened. People began to respond differently. They started agreeing with me, *"You are beautiful"*, or greeting me with warmth and affirmation: *"Hello, beautiful. How are you today?"*

It wasn't just the words that changed; it was the energy. The way they saw me mirrored the way I had finally learned to see myself.

Not everyone understood. Some scoffed. Some felt uncomfortable, even threatened. But many were inspired. My newfound confidence gave others permission to see the beauty in themselves.

It wasn't about vanity or pride. It was about truth. Because God created us all beautiful.

Another affirmation I would repeat was, *"I am a fit 130 pounds."*

A couple of months later, I was strolling down the street when I spotted one of those little free libraries, you know, the kind that looks like a birdhouse for bookworms. I decided to peek inside, half expecting to find a mystery novel or an old cookbook. But sitting right there, as if waiting just for me, was a book titled *Weigh Down Basics: The Basics to Permanent Weight Loss*. I had to laugh. I thought, *Okay, Lord, I see what You doing!*

That was August of 2017. By March of 2018, I was, indeed, a fit 130 pounds, just like I had declared.

**"I am a world renowned best selling author."**

But the real transformation wasn't just physical. For the first time, I understood what had been missing in all my past relationships. It wasn't the wrong partners or bad timing. It was *me*. I had believed the lies. All of the things I was taught about myself were all lies and I believed them.

I didn't love me, and because I didn't love me, no one else truly could. People treat you the way you treat you. I couldn't fully love anyone else, because Scripture says, *"Love your neighbor as yourself."* The most I could ever give another person was the amount of love I had for me, which was in the negatives.

More than that, I had kept *God* lingering on the outskirts of my life, always present, always patient, but never really invited into the center. I had given Him the role of a spectator, like an extra in the movie of my life. He was there in the background, waiting for His cue, while I tried to direct every scene on my own. Just like a fair-weather friend, I only handed Him a script when I was in trouble, when the drama got too heavy or the plot started falling apart. Then suddenly, I wanted Him front and center.

I hadn't nurtured my *vertical* relationship with God or my *internal* relationship with myself. Without those two, no other relationship could ever thrive. So, I got serious. I didn't just pray, I *pressed in.* I started fasting. My prayers grew deeper, more intentional, more honest. I began writing them down, making lists of people to pray for, and confronting every piece of "ugly" I could find in me.

I had to admit something that stung: how much it hurt to see one of my friends living the life I had always dreamed of, married for over twenty years, raising beautiful daughters in a home filled with love and stability. I was so jealous, I couldn't understand why my own family hadn't accepted me, or why that kind of peace always seemed just beyond my reach.

God answered.

*"This is the journey I carved out for you,"* He said. *"If they had accepted you, you would have become like them."*

He spoke to me with such tenderness that it reached the rawest parts of my soul. He reminded me that I wasn't alone in my suffering. He showed me Job, who lost everything, his family, his wealth, his health, only to find that his faith had survived the fire.

He showed me Joseph, betrayed by his brothers and sold into slavery, yet still chosen for greatness. He showed me David, the man after His own heart, who had fallen into sin so deep that redemption seemed impossible, yet mercy still found him. He showed me Naomi, who believed her life was over after losing everything, only to discover restoration in an unexpected place.

As I listened, the weight of my pain didn't disappear, but I began to *see it differently.* None of it had been wasted; not the heartbreak, not the betrayal. Not the sin that haunted me. Every tear, every scar, every valley had been woven into something greater.

I realized then: I wasn't being punished. I was being *prepared.* But of course, Satan wasn't about to let me go without a fight. He wasn't relenting, not yet.

Two years after I had moved almost an hour away, to a different county, trying to escape the ghosts of my past,

I came home to find him sitting on my porch. My heart dropped.

Randall offered some excuse about needing closure, about being hurt that I had told people I never wanted to see him again. But I knew better. This wasn't about closure. It was about access. He wasn't seeking peace, he was seeking a foothold. An opening. A way back in.

In no uncertain terms, I told him to get off my porch and out of my life. As Randall drove away for the last time, I gave him the only words that still held power between us: *"Forget you know me."*

The next day at church, true to his calling, Bishop Walker preached right to my very soul, from Exodus 14:5-31, the passage where Pharaoh changes his mind after releasing the Israelites and chases them down with his army. It was like he was picking up right where he had left off on New Year's Eve 2014 when he said, *"Get out of Egypt."* This time when he said, *"Pharaoh don't love you!"* I knew I was right where I was supposed to be.

\*\*\*

Yes, I still believe in love. However,… what matters above all is that my life, my heart, my spirit, my every intention, is fully aligned with God. My vertical relationship with Him must be unshakable, unwavering, and at the center of everything I do. I want to be so anchored in Him that the only way a man can ever truly find me is through Him. I will not settle for anything less, nor will I seek any path outside of His perfect plan. I believe, as Derek Prince so powerfully teaches in his book *God Is a Matchmaker*, that God is the ultimate matchmaker. I trust that He knows the right time, the right person, and the perfect way to bring that match together. I am willing to wait for His divine orchestration, confident that if He does not bring someone into my life, it is still exactly as it should be. His timing is perfect, and His plan is enough.

## CHAPTER 15

# FINALLY HOME

*"For this world is not our permanent home; we are looking forward to a home yet to come."* **~Hebrews 13:14**

Jeremiah came home. When he came to visit for Christmas in 2017, he looked me in the eye and said with a quiet, unshakable conviction I had never heard before, *"Mom, I'm not going back. I don't care what y'all do to me. I'm not going back."*

There was something in his tone that stopped me cold, a strength that came not from rebellion, but from pain and resolve. I knew in that moment I had to act. I found an attorney and filed for emergency custody. In court, we presented evidence of educational neglect. Patrick had failed to set up our son's Individualized Education Plan, despite his autism spectrum diagnosis. We also provided testimony about physical abuse, including an incident where Patrick had allegedly choked him.

The truth was undeniable. Patrick's wife was a longtime schoolteacher whose career could be jeopardized by these allegations so they conceded. The judge granted me sole custody. Patrick had given Jeremiah a PlayStation for Christmas, and Jeremiah had brought it with him from Memphis. But in court, because he was giving up custody, Patrick demanded that the PlayStation be returned to him. He took back his son's gift, because he could no longer have his son. That was the last of his painful and foolish attacks.

Three years later, when Jeremiah graduated from high school, Patrick and his wife attended the ceremony. It was the first time in a long time that we stood in the same space without anger. I took that opportunity to apologize, to acknowledge my part in the turmoil that had consumed us for so many years. My hands weren't completely clean, and I knew it. But I also knew I had done what I believed I needed to do to protect my child.

For a while, I thought the war was over. Patrick even came to our family reunion, and for the first time, we had real, honest conversations about our son's future. It felt like peace might finally be possible.

But life is not always so kind.

My brilliant, beautiful boy, Jeremiah, lost his way. His battle with mental health led him into the shadows of substance abuse, and eventually, into a darkness he couldn't find his way out of. In the end, he made the heartbreaking decision to leave this world.

Even in the midst of that unimaginable loss, Patrick still could not release his resentment. When it came time to make arrangements for Jeremiah's funeral, he refused to help plan or pay. Instead, he picked another fight, blocking my calls, refusing to communicate, and ensuring neither he nor his wife attended the service.

But that... that is between him and God. My hands are clean. Although my heart will always ache for my son, I have learned to rest in the promise that he is no longer suffering. I picture him now, whole and free, standing in the radiant light of a Father who never fails. God has shown me that even in the deepest grief, love does not end, it simply changes form. What was once pain has become purpose; what was once loss has become legacy.

I still feel Jeremiah's presence in quiet moments, the warmth of his smile in a stranger's kindness, the echo of his laughter in my spirit when I pray. Through it all, God has remained faithful. I may not understand His ways, but I trust His heart. I know that one day, when this journey is over, I will see my son, and my daughter again, whole, healed, and finally home.

***

Today, I work as a Certified Peer Recovery Specialist (CPRS). "A CPRS is a person who has lived the experience of a mental illness, substance use disorder, or co-occurring disorder, who has made the journey from illness to wellness, and who now wishes to help others."

My life's journey has taken me through valleys most would never imagine walking through and back again, not once, but many times. I've known loss that shatters, choices that wound, and seasons that strip away everything you thought you knew about yourself. Yet it was in those ashes that I discovered grace, real, transforming grace. Every scar has become a testimony, every failure a lesson, every heartbreak a reminder that nothing is wasted when placed in God's hands. Today, when I sit with someone in their own brokenness, I see the reflection of where I've been, and I remind them that no story is too far gone, no wound too deep, no soul too lost for God to heal. Brokenness does not cancel purpose, and redemption is not just possible, it's promised to those willing to rise again.

# EPILOGUE

Marriage is one of the most sacred covenants established by God. It is not merely a social contract or emotional arrangement; it is a divine bond meant to reflect Christ's relationship with His Church. Yet, when entered into without His guidance, even something as holy as marriage can become a source of sin and suffering. This truth has become the centerpiece of my personal journey, a journey of repeated marriages, painful divorces, and a hard-earned understanding of what it truly means to live in and outside the will of God.

**Adultery: A Covenant Broken, Not Just a Bed Defiled**

Most people think of adultery as an act of physical unfaithfulness. But when God spoke to Israel, He often accused them of adultery not because of physical betrayal but because they broke their covenant with Him. In *Jeremiah 3:8*, the Lord says:

*"I gave faithless Israel her certificate of divorce and sent her away because of all her adulteries."*

Adultery, then, is not simply the act of infidelity, it is any violation of covenant. When we make vows before God and break them through disobedience, rebellion, or idolatry, we are guilty of spiritual adultery. Whether in marriage or in faith, to go against the terms of a sacred promise is to wound the heart of God.

This understanding reshaped how I viewed my own life. My cheating, my fear of abandonment, my search for love, all of it revealed not only broken relationships with men but also a broken covenant with God. I was seeking fulfillment from relationships that were never rooted in His will. The real adultery began when I chose my own desires over God's direction.

**Divorce: A Hard Reality, Not a Forbidden Door**

The Bible's stance on divorce is complex, yet profoundly intentional. In *Matthew 19:9*, Jesus teaches:

*"I tell you that anyone who divorces his wife, except for sexual immorality, and marries another woman commits adultery."*

Many stop reading there, assuming that divorce is never acceptable except for unfaithfulness. But Scripture also reveals moments when divorce was necessary to restore righteousness, particularly when the marriage itself was outside of God's will.

In *Ezra 10*, the people of Israel realized they had sinned by marrying foreign women against God's command. Their response was not to remain in those relationships but to repent and *separate* themselves:

*"We have been unfaithful to our God by marrying foreign women from the peoples around us. But in spite of this, there is still hope for Israel. Now let us make a covenant*

*before our God to send away all these women and their children." Ezra 10:2–3*

That passage really resonated with me. These were not divorces born out of pride or selfishness, they were acts of repentance. The Israelites had entered unions God never ordained, and in order to realign themselves with Him, they had to let go. In that moment of revelation, I realized that sometimes the sin is not the divorce, but the marriage itself.

**Marrying Outside the Will of God**

Every marriage I entered into, was born from selfish desire, fear, or loneliness, not divine instruction. I married because I wanted to be a wife and mother. I married because I didn't want to live in sin. I married because I refused to be someone's "permanent girlfriend." I married to prove my worth and to silence the voice that told me no one would ever want me. I even married out of fear, fear of dying alone, a thought that has haunted me since I was eight years old.

But none of those reasons align with God's purpose for marriage. A covenant made out of fear is not faith; it is self-preservation. And what I learned through painful repetition is that every time I acted outside of God's will, the union was doomed from the start. The foreign marriages of Ezra 10 symbolize more than ancient Israel's disobedience, they represent every relationship we enter that God did not authorize. Such relationships, however sincere, cannot stand under the weight of divine truth.

**Life Lesson: Realignment Through Repentance**

When the Israelites realized their sin, they did not justify it or try to make it work. They repented, realigned, and obeyed. Likewise, when I faced the truth of my choices, I had to confront my motives and the reality that my marriages were not ordained by God. I began to understand that repentance is not merely apologizing, but turning away from what God never blessed.

God's mercy is vast, but His standards do not bend. In *2 Corinthians 6:14*, Paul warns:

*"Do not be unequally yoked with unbelievers. For what partnership has righteousness with lawlessness?"*

Marrying outside of God's will is not just about faith differences, it's about disobedience. When we choose partners, careers, or paths that conflict with His plan, we invite spiritual struggle and demonic influence into our lives. Ezra 10 reminds us that restoration often requires release.

**A Final Reflection: The Covenant Restored**

Today, I no longer view divorce as the ultimate failure, for me, it was the painful doorway back to God's will. The real tragedy was not the ending of the marriages but the beginning of what never should have been. When we step outside of divine instruction, we forfeit peace. When we return through repentance, we regain covenant.

This epilogue is *not* an invitation to abandon your marriage. Let me say that plainly and emphatically: **DO NOT** divorce your spouse on my account. Rather, it is a call to examine the foundation upon which your union was built. Was it built on fear, convenience, or loneliness, or was it built on God's word? Every covenant must be tested by the question: *Is this God's will for me?*

In *Hosea 2:19*, God says to His people:

*"I will make you my wife forever, showing you righteousness and justice, unfailing love and compassion."*

This is the marriage God desires with us. A covenant rooted in His righteousness, guided by His word, and sustained by His Spirit.

I leave you with this: Before you promise yourself to another, promise yourself to God. Let Him be your first covenant, your eternal spouse, and your guiding voice. For only through Him can any other union truly stand.

# REFLECTION & DISCUSSION QUESTIONS

1. How does your understanding of adultery change when viewed as a breaking of covenant rather than just physical infidelity?

   _____

   _____

2. In what ways might fear, loneliness, or pressure influence our decisions about marriage or relationships?

   _____

   _____

3. How does Ezra 10 challenge your perspective on divorce and repentance?

   _____

   _____

4. What does it mean to marry or partner "outside of the will of God" in a modern context?

   _____

   _____

5. Have you taken time to ask God if your current or past relationships were aligned with His will?

_____

_____

6. What practical steps can you take to ensure that your next covenant, whether with a spouse, a ministry, a friend or a purpose, is guided by God's direction rather than emotion?

_____

_____

7. How can you strengthen your covenant relationship with God today?

_____

_____

**Life Application:** Spend time in prayer this week asking God to reveal any area of your life where you have made a covenant outside of His will. Seek His guidance to realign yourself through repentance, forgiveness, and faith. Remember: repentance is not punishment, it's restoration. Until we meet again…

**Be Amazing!**

www.ingramcontent.com/pod-product-compliance
Lightning Source LLC
LaVergne TN
LVHW040057080526
838202LV00045B/3671